VALUES IN SOCIAL WORK

To Liz, Megan and Cerian

Values in Social Work

Second Edition

MICHAEL HORNE

Ashgate
ARENA

Aldershot • Brookfield USA • Singapore • Sydney

Published by
Ashgate Publishing Ltd
Gower House
Croft Road
Aldershot
Hants GU11 3HR
England

Ashgate Publishing Company
Old Post Road
Brookfield
Vermont 05036
USA

Ashgate website: http://www.ashgate.com

British Library Cataloguing in Publication Data
Horne, Michael, 1953–
    Values in social work. – 2nd ed.
    1. Social service – Moral and ethical aspects – Great
    Britain
    I. Title
    361.3'2

Library of Congress Cataloging-in-Publication Data
Horne, Michael, 1953–
    Values in social work / Michael Horne. – 2nd ed.
        p.   cm.
    Includes bibliographical references and index.
    ISBN 1-85742-329-1 (hardback). – ISBN 1-85742-330-5 (pbk.)
    1. Social service–Moral and ethical aspects.   2. Social service–
Great Britain.   I. Title.
HV40.H66   1999
361'.941–dc21
                                                                                    99-41124
                                                                                    CIP

ISBN 1 85742 329 1 (HBK)
ISBN 1 85742 330 5 (PBK)

Typeset by Manton Typesetters, Louth, Lincolnshire, UK.
Printed and bound by Athenaeum Press, Ltd., Gateshead, Tyne & Wear.

Contents

Preface to the second edition

This second edition of *Values in Social Work* consists of and develops the examination of the underlying values that inform and guide social work practice – particularly focusing on 'respect for persons' and 'client self-determination' – that was begun in the first edition.

Social work is a complex activity. As a profession it purports to be guided by a code of ethics, established by its professional body/association, which encompasses a set of 'commonly' held, liberal, humanitarian beliefs. These beliefs, in the form of a code of ethics, are intended to guide the nature of the relationship between the social worker and client/user, to 'protect' the client whilst reminding the social worker of her 'societal' responsibilities. These expectations of social workers are both complex and far from unambiguous. At the very least they raise important questions regarding possible conflicts of interests that the social worker may be faced with. In order to understand this situation, one is immediately thrown into examining the nature, role and task of social work in society.

Identifying and explaining the role of values in social work, that is, in actual practice, is an area of study which has not received the attention that it deserves, either in terms of research, theorising or teaching. Traditionally, 'theorizing' has tended either to examine social work values within the too narrow parameters of the client/social worker relationship, largely ignoring the social forces that brought them together; or, at the other end of the spectrum, to identify only the structural dimensions of social work in society, ignoring the dynamics and effect of this on the actual role and relationship between the social worker and client.

I attempted to address this situation in the first edition of *Values in Social Work*. This revised second edition takes this examination further by developing a closer examination of both the processes by which society identifies certain people and groups as 'worthy' of social work attention, and the ways in which the values of social work are actually used in both confirming certain people as 'clients', or as being part of a process in which these 'clientizing' processes can potentially be challenged.

In the preface to the first edition of *Values in Social Work*, I identified the main emphasis of the book as seeking to understand values in social work primarily from the perspective of local authority-based social work practice. There were two principal reasons for this.

First, my own social work practice (residential and field-based) continually generated questions related to values in social work: for example, why the idea of client self-determination does not always seem to be very prominent (if recognisable at all) in practice. Philosophically-based texts told me a great deal about the concept of self-determination, but little or nothing about its relevance and place in actual social work practice.

Second, and closely related to the first reason, is the need to examine practice, to understand what the social workers do, and why they do it. As a social worker, what I did often did not seem to be in accord with the textbooks (perhaps a reflection on my practice as much as a comment on the textbooks). The 'reality' often was much more complex, with more variables, possibilities and restrictions. Put together, these two reasons explain why I saw a need for and engaged in a study of values in social work from a 'practice'-based perspective. This perspective maintains its central position in this second edition.

The overall aim of this book is to present a 'critical' (and perhaps in places, 'provocative') perspective on social work values that hopefully will encourage in the reader their own examination of social work values.

Finally, it is hoped that this second edition of *Values in Social Work* comprises a useful addition to a much welcome growing body of literature on social work values.

Michael Horne
University of York, January 1999

Acknowledgements

I would first like to thank the social workers who kindly and bravely agreed to be interviewed, for both the first edition and this second edition of *Values in Social Work*. Their contribution plays a central part in this book, in terms of the case material presented, and for the insights into social work practice that they have shared with me. I would also like to express my continuing gratitude to Martin Davies and David Howe for the support and encouragement that they gave me whilst I was a student at the University of East Anglia, beginning my interest in social work values.

Thanks are also due to the many colleagues and social work students who have listened to and challenged my thinking over the years.

Introduction

Social work is a professional activity. Implicit in its practice are ethical principles which prescribe the professional responsibility of the social worker. The primary objective of the code of ethics is to make these implicit principles explicit for the protection of clients and other members of society. (BASW 1996, para. 1)

Competence in social work requires the understanding and integration of the values of social work. (CCETSW 1989, p. 15)

Ethical issues are at the heart of a discipline such as social work. (Hugman and Smith 1995, p. 1)

Social workers regularly confront practice dilemmas: the necessity to take difficult decisions, in which there are no right answers, based on a delicate assessment of risk and competing (if not conflicting) rights: and a myriad of pressures, including from within. The result is a complex maze and interaction of personal, professional, interagency and societal dynamics and pressures and potential tangles between service users, social workers, agencies and society. (Preston-Shoot and Agass 1900, p. 10)

Social work as a value-laden activity

There are a number of different ways in which values and ethics have been written about and identified as central to social work, as the quotes above suggest. This centrality is evidenced in the development of a professional code of ethics for social workers by the British Association of Social Workers (BASW), which identifies the nature of the responsibilities of social workers. This in turn is supported by the Central Council for Education and Training in Social Work (CCETSW) through the identification of the significance and need to integrate the values that underpin social work in the education and training of social workers at both qualifying and post-qualifying levels.

The quotes above also indicate something of the complexities of social work practice, in which social workers may often find themselves grappling with competing and sometimes conflicting responsibilities and expectations, behind which lie different value priorities and demands – from personal, professional, agency and societal perspectives. Who is identified as a client, how they are identified as such, and the response and role of the social worker in working with that person are all infused with value-based assessments and judgements.

Similarly, an examination of social work from the perspective of its knowledge base, which is largely derived from the social sciences, also strongly supports the idea of social work as a value-laden activity. Despite the skills which it espouses as affording it 'technical' or 'scientific' validity, they do not remove from within its practice the necessity of making evaluative judgements and decisions:

> Without entering into the heated controversy over the degree of objectivity in the social sciences, all would surely agree that in the case of social work, a value system (more often than not couched in terms of social and political ideology) forms the general framework of decision making within which the social worker defines both his overall role and his specific course of action. (Pritchard and Taylor 1978, p. 70)

To seek and yearn for an expertise in human relationships, as Downie and Telfer argue, with the aim of denying the 'value-reality' of social work is illusory: 'No amount of knowledge of what is the case can ever establish for us what we ought to do about it' (1980, p. 22). Levy also describes social work as a value-based profession, when he describes social work as 'not only a way of doing something, but a constellation of preferences concerning what merits doing and how it should be done' (1976, p. 238).

'Value talk' in social work

Timms (1983, p. 24) identifies three main ways in which social work values are written about. First, they appear in the form of generalised accounts of 'value' or 'values' (for example, classically, Biestek 1974). Second, they are the subject of essays (or collections of essays) which offer some critical assessment of a 'value' or 'values' (for example, McDermott 1975, Hugman and Smith 1995). Third, they may be subject to some form of empirical investigation, which studies social work values in a more direct manner (for example, McLeod and Meyer 1967).

Both the 'literature'-based approach, and the 'empirically'-based approach have been criticized for their tendency to fall into the trap of routinely listing what are taken to be social work values, and for their lack of conceptual analysis of the nature and form of these values, for example:

> ... the tendency in social work literature to list routinely and indiscriminately a series of so-called social work values as if nothing more need to be said for all to understand ... They [social workers] are so accustomed to citing these items, almost by rote, that no explanation seems necessary – and certainly not from one another. This may be one of the reasons for the limited progress in coping with professional value issues. (Levy 1973, p. 34)

Similarly, Timms (1983) criticizes the social work literature for not treating the subject of social work values, and 'values' problems with sufficient 'rigour' and 'conceptualization':

> 'Value' appears frequently in social work literature, but value talk is underdeveloped and conversation about values or social work values has hardly started. This is mainly because it is assumed that everyone knows what values (or beliefs, or ethics, or philosophy, or attitudes, or preferences) are; that is, a value is a value; and that values may be elaborated, but cannot be argued about. (1983, p. 32)

Whilst this criticism accurately reflects the superficial way in which social work values and the language of values have, and often still are referred to and used, it is worth noting that in recent years the values and ethics underpinning social work have been the subject of a small number of serious and critical examinations. The first edition of this book (Horne 1987), Reamer (1990), Jamal (1994), Banks (1995) and Hugman and Smith (1995) are all examples of a more 'rigorous' approach to the subject area.

Empirical research on social work values has also been criticized for its tendency to compile lists and for its inadequate attention to conceptual analysis of the values it lists. Research studies into social work values have not been numerous, the most well known being that of Pumphrey (1959), McLeod and Meyer (1967) and Channon (1974). Timms (1983, p. 28) describes such empirical work that has so far been carried out as 'premature in so far as its grasp on "value" is hesitant and clumsy'. In his criticism of Pumphrey, and McLeod and Meyer, he argues that they lack 'conceptual exploration'. For example, regarding McLeod and Meyer's research, he writes, 'It is not easy to avoid the judgement that more conceptual preparation would have produced a better result' (1983, p. 28). With respect to Pumphrey's research, he argues that he failed to analyse possible problems and conflicts inherent in the application of values in practice: 'Protective activity might sometimes clash with the client's right of self-determination, whilst suffering could be said to be part of the "reality" which social workers quite often believe they should assist their clients to face' (Timms 1970, p. 120).

Timms goes on to suggest that what is needed is a study of social work values, based on what social workers actually do when faced with a choice between 'valued' courses of action, rather than studies based on what social workers mention or list as being important: 'The question to ask is not so much what things, concepts, states of affairs, do social workers value, but how much do they value them?' (1970, p. 120). Similarly in 1983 (p. 32) he writes: 'We should just attend more closely and critically to the literature and also to the problems of the social worker making choices.'

What social workers actually 'do' and 'why' is the central focus of *Values in Social Work*.

BASW and CCETSW

Though it is the case that there has been a general lack of critical examination and conceptual analysis of social work values, it is also true that they are extremely difficult to clearly identify in a form that provides a clear 'ethical' guide to professional social work practice. This difficulty is very much apparent when one examines the British Association of Social Workers' (BASW) *A Code of Ethics for Social Work*:

> Social work is a professional activity. Implicit in its practice are ethical principles which prescribe the professional responsibility of the social worker. The primary objective of the code of ethics is to make these implicit principles explicit for the protection of clients and other members of society. (BASW 1996, para 1)

This opening statement in the code of ethics raises a number of problems or questions. By stating at the outset that 'social work is a professional activity', it seems to ignore the important point that a set of ethical principles for social work should start with a consideration (or at least an acknowledgement) of the responsibilities of the social worker (made by Fairbairn 1985, p. 86). In the *Code* this 'unqualified' description of social work as a 'profession' is followed up by a call for a code of ethics 'for the protection of clients and other members of society'.

It could be argued that social work as a profession is severely limited, because certainly in Britain, social workers are accountable to the authority of their employers (state or independent agencies) in the first place rather than to their clients for their decisions. If, as Payne argues, a code of ethics is based on the idea of professional responsibility to, and for the protection of clients (1985, p. 102), how can it, and does it, also accommodate responsibility to an employer, and 'other members of society'?

To be fair, the *Code* does recognize this 'dilemma' by stating in paragraph 3 that social workers are responsible to 'their clients, to their employers, to each other, to colleagues in other disciplines, and to society'; in the commentary, it states that it is an oversimplification to say that either clients or employers should take precedence. However, this immediately raises the question of what does the social worker do, or what are the 'ethical' criteria for deciding what to do, if one or more of the significant parties in a particular case are in conflict? Crucially the *Code* does not suggest how possible conflicts of interest and responsibility which the social worker might face, be resolved.

From this, it does seem that as a guide for practice, the code is inadequate, even at a very general level. However, it is perhaps rather harsh at this stage to condemn as inadequate BASW's *Code of Ethics* because of this, without first examining in more detail some of the complexities of the nature and role of social work practice. Again, in examining what social workers 'do', and 'why', these complexities are examined in this book.

In identifying the structure and content of social work training at qualifying and post-qualifying levels, the Central Council for the Education and Training in Social Work (CCETSW) has emphasized the centrality of values to social work practice. In the paper issued by CCETSW on training in social work, it is stated that:

> It is fundamental that education and training leading to a qualification award should aim to equip social workers with the professional values and ethics which must guide their work and their accountability, and which they need in order to act as part of a wider professional group. Given that at present most social workers in this country are employed in public services, the nature and purposes of which are by definition politically determined, it is important that qualifying education and training should provide the opportunity for social work students to learn about the roles and responsibilities of professional employed in public, voluntary, and private bureaucratic structures, and to be clear about the values and ethics espoused by their profession. (CCETSW 1985, p. 9)

Once again, this is a confused and rather evasive statement, primarily in that it offers no recognition of the possibility of conflict between 'social work values and ethics', to which it says social workers are accountable, and their employers, whose 'nature and purposes are "politically determined"'. With specific reference to the Diploma in Social Work CCETSW have stated:

Since values are integral to rather than separate from competent practice, evidence that value requirements have been met, must be drawn from and refer to specific practice undertaken in relation to the six core competencies. It is clear, consistent and thoughtful integration of values in practice, that students must demonstrate and programme providers seek evidence of in all assessable work. (CCETSW 1995, p. 4)

The 'Values Requirements' listed by CCETSW that students must demonstrate are:

- Identify and question their own values and prejudices, and their implications for practice.
- Respect and value uniqueness and diversity, and recognize and build on strengths.
- Promote people's rights to choice, privacy, confidentiality and protection, while recognizing and addressing the complexities of competing rights and demands.
- Assist people to increase control of and improve the quality of their lives, while recognizing that control of behaviour will be required at times in order to protect children and adults from harm.
- Identify, analyse and take action to counter discrimination, racism, disadvantage, inequality and injustice, using strategies appropriate to role and context.
- Practise in a manner that does not stigmatize or disadvantage either individuals, groups or communities. (CCETSW 1995, p. 4)

This list of values covers a wide range of expectations of (student) social workers that relate not only to the relationship between themselves and the client, which itself is by no means necessarily straightforward, but also identify the wider political and societal issues that provide the context of that relationship, which the social worker must also address. As with the BASW *Code of Ethics*, these expectations contain many potential areas of conflict of interests and priorities between the significant agents involved.

From this introductory exploration of values in social work, it is evident that this is a complex area of enquiry from a number of important perspectives, which are examined in the following sections: what do social workers do'?; 'who' is the client?; 'what is the nature of the relationship between the social worker and client?' are all questions infused with value-based expectations, dilemmas and questions.

Aims

The aim of the book is to examine social work values – what they are, what they mean – and understand them in the context of social work practice in Britain. This is done in three parts.

Part I consists of a critical examination of 'respect for persons' and 'client self-determination'. These are identified as the underpinning values that inform the relationship between the social worker and the client, and which (in theory at least) recognize and protect the 'rights' of the client within this relationship. Both 'respect for persons' and 'client self-determination' raise some critical issues however, which will be addressed in this section. This examination necessarily leads to a number of questions about whether 'respect for persons' is an appropriate or adequate baseline ethic for social work. Also raised are questions about what actually happens to social work values in practice? How, and in what ways, do they inform the relationship between the social worker and client, and the role of the social worker?

Part II, addresses these questions through two detailed case studies that illustrate something of what happens to values in social work practice. In relation to Timms' comments quoted earlier, the case studies show, by describing and analysing cases in detail, what social workers do, and how their values 'work' in practice. Whilst Part I focuses mainly on the relationship between the social worker and the client, Part II begins to look at and illustrates how that relationship is determined and affected by 'outside factors'; for example, by the demands of agency function and society's expectations, which itself raises further questions regarding our understanding of social work values and the nature and function of social work in society.

Part III follows on from this by presenting a theoretical framework which gives a description of social work that accommodates and examines the nature of the social worker's relationships with both the individual and with society, and offers an understanding of social work values in this context. Part III attempts to analyse and clarify what are often left in 'value talk' as vague (or in the case of BASW's *Code of Ethics*, potentially contradictory as well) references to the social worker's responsibilities to individuals (clients) and to society.

Part I

Values in theory

'Value talk' in social work often consists of lists of what it is considered the moral or ethical principles of social work are, or should be. These are often referred to 'traditional', 'classic' or 'decontextualised' lists (Hugman and Smith 1995, p. 3) in that they are an attempt to elucidate a set of basic universal ethical principles upon which social work is based. Whilst the lists vary, there are generally strong similarities between them. Timms (1983, p. 46) gives five typical inclusions in a 'value list':

1 To respect the client.
2 To accept 'him' for 'himself'.
3 Not to condemn 'him'.
4 To uphold 'his' right to self-determination.
5 To respect 'his' confidence.

Butrym (1976, Ch. 3) describes three fundamental assumptions on which social work is based:

1 Respect for persons.
2 'A belief in the social nature of "man" as a unique creature depending on other "men" for fulfilment of his uniqueness' (p. 45).
3 'A belief in the human capacity for change, growth and betterment' (p. 45).

From these 'values of a very high order of abstraction' (p. 47) she then lists six 'middle-range conceptualisations of moral principles', based on Biestek's classification (1974), that are directly relevant to social work practice:

1 Acceptance
2 Non-judgmental attitude
3 Individualization
4 The 'purposeful expression of feelings' and 'controlled emotional involvement'
5 Confidentiality
6 Self-determination

The analysis below concentrates on 'respect for persons'. Basically all other social work values are derived from, and are a part of the meaning of, this ethical principle. This will be followed by an analysis of the value the 'client's right to self-determination', which is one of the central principles (as far as social work is concerned) that is derived from 'respect for persons', and which is also one of the most contentious and open to debate regarding its applicability (and limits) in contemporary social work practice.

Judging from the brief lists offered above, this approach most obviously ignores (at least explicitly) the value of 'respecting the client's confidence', which appears in Timms' and Butrym's lists, and also the purposeful expression of feelings and 'controlled emotional involvement' from Butrym's 'middle-range' list. All the other values are expressions of 'respect of persons' and 'client self-determination', which itself indicates the centrality of these two values in providing a value-base to social work. Because of this the following analysis of the social work 'value' literature and theory concentrates on these two values. Also, by focusing on respect for persons and client self-determination we are able to identify a number of critical questions about the efficacy of social work's ethical base.

1 Respect for persons

The concept of 'respect for persons' is fundamental to most discussions of values in social work literature, both as a moral principle from which other principles are derived, and as a prerequisite for morality itself. One of the most influential writers on social work values has been Raymond Plant, who describes respect for persons as 'not just a moral principle, on the contrary it is a presupposition of having the concept of a moral principle at all' (Plant 1970, p. 20). Plant goes on to say that other values, such as self-determination, are implicit in 'respect for persons'. (I will discuss whether or not this is the case in the next chapter.) Downie and Telfer, two influential writers on social work values, go even further than Plant: ' ... the attitude of "respect for persons" is morally basic ... not only is it the paramount moral attitude, but also ... all other moral principles and attitudes are to be explained in terms of it' (Downie and Telfer 1969, p. 33).

As far as its fundamental importance to social work practice is concerned, the following quote from BASW illustrates what it sees to be the practical implications of 'respect for persons':

> Basic to the profession of social work is the recognition of the value and dignity of every human being irrespective of origin, race, status, sex, sexual orientation, age, disability, belief or contribution to society. The profession accepts responsibility to encourage and facilitate the self-realisation of the individual person with due regard for the interest of others. (BASW 1996, para. 6)

Plant himself indicates that in relation to social work practice, the values of individualization, acceptance and self-direction (self-determination) are in fact implicit in 'respect for persons': 'They are deductions from this concept in that they are part of its very meaning. Respect for persons is, on this view, the basic value of casework' (Plant 1970, p. 11).

Ends and means

The principle of respect for persons is derived from the eighteenth-century German philosopher, Immanuel Kant. The most common way of describing what is meant by this principle is that people should be treated as ends in themselves, not as means to ends. This comes directly from the categorical imperative (a command that one should adhere to, in order to act morally) that one should 'Act in such a way that you always treat humanity, whether in your own person or in the person of any other, never simply as a means, but always at the same time as an end' (Kant in Paton 1948, p. 91).

The concept that each person is an end in herself argues for an equal evaluation of each individual which is not based on what are considered to be morally arbitrary features such as experience, ability, intelligence, social standing, or any other 'empirical' quality. Whilst every individual possesses a number of such features which help to determine her role in society; in themselves, these do not constitute her value as an end. According to 'respect for persons', such variations are arbitrary and exist on 'top of' the evaluation that each person has 'a legitimate claim to be valued equally with any others' (Budgen 1982, p. 34). Zofia Butrym describes 'respect for persons' as being 'due to the inherent worth of man [sic] and is thus independent of his actual achievements or behaviour' (Butrym 1976, p. 43).

Plant sums up this philosophy in the following quotation from Kant which he cites:

> A man deserves respect as a potential moral agent in terms of his transcendental characteristic, not because of a particular conjunction of empirical qualities which he might possess. Traits of character might command admiration and other such responses, but respect is owed to a man irrespective of what he does because he is a man. (Plant 1970, p. 12)

In other words, to treat someone as an end is to treat her as being of unconditional moral worth.

Rationality

The basis of, or justification for 'respect for persons' is, according to Kant, the individual's possession of rationality – the rational will. Before describing this, it should be pointed out that 'rationality' is not to be taken as being contrasted with 'irrationality', but with 'non-rationality'. For example, many clients come or are sent to see social workers because they are considered not to be behaving rationally. This does not mean that they are to be regarded as being irrational – rather that their ability to make rational decisions may be temporarily affected or lessened through some form of stress, crisis, illness, etc. The case of children, people with learning difficulties and people with mental health problems is more complex and will be discussed in the examination below of what and who constitutes a person (or 'personhood').

According to Kant, an individual's absolute worth comes from her possession of the rational will, which enables one to think and act in a rational manner. Budgen describes two ways in which the exercise of the 'rational will' can be seen, first by 'the ability to choose for oneself, and more extensively to formulate purposes, plans and policies of one's own' (1982, p. 34); and second, by 'the ability to carry out decisions, plans or policies without undue reliance on the help of others' (quote from Downie and Telfer 1969, p. 20). To impair a person's abilities to choose and execute her own plan is, as Downie and Telfer put it, to that extent to 'destroy' her as a person (1969, p. 21).

Autonomy

The main feature of Kant's analysis of the 'rational will' is the autonomy of the will – that is, our ability to act in the pursuit of our own self-chosen goals – to act in pursuit of our own personal conception of the 'good life'. Within our liberal, democratic society (relatively so at least), autonomy is valued very highly, both as a means to the achievement of our goals and as an end in its own right. In addition, someone who is seen as being autonomous, and as being 'independent' is also likely to be recognized as a 'worthwhile' member of society. This point is particularly pertinent in the context of social work with clients where the aim is to increase or develop the individual's ability to live independently; that is, without the assistance of social work/care support.

As Budgen, and Downie and Telfer, have pointed out, people have their own chosen purposes and projects, so to treat someone as an end is to value the individual and recognize the individual's right to live according to her purposes and projects. To treat someone solely as a 'means' would, for example, be to make a false promise to them in order to secure a loan which one had no intention of repaying.

Richard Lindley (1984) cites Aldous Huxley's novel, *Brave New World*, as an example of a society in which the majority of the people were without any autonomy, that is, they were not treated as ends in themselves. Rather, they were treated instrumentally, in that their wills were manipulated, allegedly for their own benefit. Therefore, pleasant though the Brave New World may have been for its inhabitants, it nevertheless seriously violated the Kantian principle of 'respect for persons'.

It is important to be aware that each person, as the possessor of a rational will, is able to live according to her own projects, purposes and rules, but another person may possibly live according to a different set of projects and rules. So whilst it may be morally acceptable to use rational argument to try and get the other person to change her mind, it would be morally wrong (that is, a denial of her as a person?) to attempt to make her change her mind by the exercise of power, coercion or manipulation. On a strict interpretation of the Kantian principle, as rational beings, we should always respect the autonomy of others. To do otherwise would be morally wrong, since the principle which justified the behaviour could not be accepted by the other person or persons, and therefore could not be 'willed to be a universal law'. The CCETSW paper on values in social work puts this in the following way:

> A rational being cannot propose to act on a principle if he cannot propose at the same time that others should act upon it. 'Man' should be seen as an end in himself; to use a person as a means by deceiving or manipulating him is to deprive him of the respect and opportunity for choice which one would expect for oneself. (CCETSW 1976, p. 22)

The obvious social work value which has its roots in this aspect of 'respect for persons' is the concept of self-determination – the ability to choose for oneself, and the ability to carry out actions and policies, etc., of one's own. (This value/concept is discussed in detail in Chapter 2.)

A further aspect of 'respecting a person' involves an awareness that certain roles, projects, values, etc., apply to everyone alike, for example, social workers and their clients. So, in helping with a client's problems, the social worker is morally bound not to do so at the expense of the social norms which apply to all.

This is interesting and potentially problematical, because it could be seen as possibly clashing with respecting a person as an autonomous (self-determining) being, which itself involves assisting the client in the pursuit of the actions and policies that she wishes to implement. Or, it may limit or deny the social worker's responsibilities to try to remove the social, economic or political (structural) impediments to the realization of their client's aspirations.

Not very helpfully in terms of resolving possible conflict, Downie and Telfer describe social work as having to cope with the rights and duties of different social roles, so that the self-determination of clients as moral agents is maximized, and balanced against the rights of others within a liberal democracy. BASW (1996) alludes to this 'reality' in its code of ethics: the principle that 'The profession accepts a responsibility to encourage and facilitate the self-realisation of each individual with due regard to the interest of others' (consistent with the notion of 'autonomy') is followed by the commentary that: 'Social workers are often concerned with trying to harmonise conflicting interests and failing harmony, to arrive at the least damaging solution for all concerned. It is therefore, sometimes not possible to ensure that there will be no detriment to the interests of others, or to the client's interest' (BASW 1996, para. 6).

'Personhood'

Central to any description of 'respect for persons', certainly within the framework of social work, is the definition of who and what constitutes a person, or 'personhood', implicit within which is the question of whether it applies to all human beings 'irrespective of origin, race, status, sex, sexual orientation, age, disability, belief or contribution to society' (BASW 1996, para. 6). For example, how does it apply to children, elderly people, people with learning difficulties, people with mental health problems, etc., who might be seen as not being able to act rationally or with autonomy?

Noel Timms (1983, p. 61) comments that some commentators see 'respect for persons' as actively promoting discrimination against those who may not count as persons, or as being 'fully persons' according to what are agreed to be the criteria of 'personhood'.

Downie and Telfer (1969, p. 35) provide a possible solution to this question of who to include as 'persons' by suggesting that 'respect' entails different emphases depending on the individual concerned. By their criteria, 'respect for persons' applied to rational individuals with full capabilities is the central case; particular individuals may approximate to this central case to a varying extent. Budgen (1982, p. 39) follows Downie and Telfer's argument through by suggesting that children can be seen as *potential* persons, the senile are *lapsed* persons, the mentally ill are *temporarily lapsed* persons, and people with learning difficulties can be considered to be *permanently potential* persons (!).

The important point is that according to Downie and Telfer (1969, p. 35) there are still sufficient resemblances between the above groups and fully 'rational' persons to justify including them in the principle of 'respect for persons'. A second aspect of their approach to 'persons' is to stress that there are possible attitudes (other than 'respect for persons') which are helpful in dealing with people in this 'minimal' sense. They suggest that affection and pity are relevant in dealing with this group of persons (as well as being relevant for dealing with fully rational persons). Whilst affection and pity in themselves are not moral attitudes, they are consistent with 'respect for persons' and can reinforce it. A final aspect of Downie and Telfer's solution to the problem of 'minimal' persons is that, all persons possess (equally) the characteristic of 'feeling', and as 'feeling' beings, all persons should be treated with 'respect for persons'.

Mentioned above was the fact that some commentators have been critical of 'respect for persons' because they see it as promoting discrimination against non-fully rational, or minimal persons. One such commentator is David Watson. Referring to 'minimal' persons, he writes:

> ... a caring profession adopting this principle [respect for persons] must stigmatise individuals not exercising these [rational] capacities ... the ability to choose for oneself etc. are hardly possessed by very young children and the senile, and not possessed at all by some severely mentally handicapped individuals; 'respect for persons' provides little or no moral reason, respectively, for the care of these individuals. We are only obliged to control them. Caring professions working with these individuals must find another principle if talk of 'caring' is to be taken seriously. (Watson 1980, pp. 59–60)

This criticism is extremely potent given that a great many users of social/care services, are those very individuals that would not be considered 'full' persons according to the criteria described above. This brings into question the efficacy of respect for persons as the underlying moral imperative for the profession of social work. At best it appears to legitimate a limited form of 'care' based on pity or affection, and at worst it provides a rational for interpreting care of and for 'minimal' persons primarily within a paradigm of control.

Watson's solution is to construct a principle of 'respect for human beings', on the grounds that this offers a wider range of characteristics than is included in 'respect for persons'. Watson comments that 'respect for human beings' could entail 'valuing the capacity to be emotionally secure, the desire to give and the capacity to receive love and affection, as well as the distinctive endowments of a human being' (1980, p. 61).

However, it is not at all clear just what Watson's replacement of 'persons' by 'human beings' actually introduces that could not be accommodated within 'respect for persons' itself. As Budgen states, 'though "respect for persons" assumes choosers one can see it as capable of generalisation to the problem groups ... such a the confused elderly' (1982, p. 40).

The distinction which Watson makes between 'respect for persons' and 'respect for human beings' appears to be arbitrary. There is no logical disjunction (or at least not one explained by Watson) between the quality of, or needs of 'persons' and the quality of, or needs of 'human beings'. However, this does not actually constitute an argument against the criticism that non-fully rational 'persons' or 'human beings' are treated with less respect than fully rational persons. In fact, the later discussion of self-determination as positive freedom will suggest that within social work (which might be described as specializing in non-fully rational persons; or persons that society defines as such), such discrimination does exist.

Autonomy and paternalism

Obviously, the inclusion of 'minimal persons' in the principle of respect for persons has important implications for social work, not the least being the consideration of the relationship between autonomy or self-determination and paternalism. It can be plausibly argued that a principle of paternalism can be, or even needs to be, developed which recognizes the need to intervene to protect the welfare and interests of 'minimal' persons. Noel Timms describes paternalism as involving 'a turning of someone away from his [sic] current preferences or judgements; and the use of a particular kind of justification, generally along the lines that the intervention was in the others' interest, or actually furthered his welfare' (1983, p. 63).

Husak (1981) argues that a paternalistic relationship is necessarily built on a relationship of inferiority–superiority: 'Hence a lack of rationality, prudence, foresight, intelligence, maturity, or some other deficiency or shortcoming in which the alleged inferiority consists, seems necessary before paternalistic treatment could be thought appropriate' (1981, p. 40).

As far as the principle of respect for persons in concerned, it is claimed that by acting in what are perceived to be the best interests of the client, the social worker is able to claim that she is operating within the conditions of the principle. However, in this form, it does appear that the individual's autonomy is potentially open to manipulation. It would also appear to be stretching the meaning and application of Kant's maxim that one should respect the autonomy of all parties, since to do otherwise would mean that the maxim could not be 'willed to be universal law' in the appropriate sense. Interpreted in this strict way, the Kantian 'respect for persons' appears to be inconsistent with the concept of paternalism, since the latter necessarily requires some degree of manipulation. The apparent implausibility of Kant's principle which this argument highlights (in respect of its applicability to social work at least) can be illustrated by the following example.

If one saw a child standing at the kerbside, about to step into the road directly into the path of an approaching vehicle, one would have no hesitation in reaching out to stop the child in order to save her from serious, or perhaps fatal injury. By doing so one would be intervening paternalistically (by definition without the child's consent) in restricting the child's planned action (of stepping into the road); that is, one would be violating the child's autonomy. Strictly speaking, it might be argued that one would be violating the Kantian principle (given Downie and Telfer's inclusion of 'minimal' persons in the principle). However, by such an intervention, it could be rightly argued that by saving the child from injury (possibly fatal), one was in fact protecting the child's ability to remain a (potentially in the first instance, according to Downie and Telfer) rational, autonomous individual.

The important consideration here is that as individuals we exist through time and our long-term interests (for example, not getting run over by large vehicles) may sometimes conflict with our short-term interests (for example, crossing roads at particular points in time). Certainly as far as the above illustration is concerned 'respect for persons' should prescribe that one acts to promote a person's long-term interests, even at the expense of violating their autonomy or self-determination in the short term.

Richard Lindley (1984), in his discussion of strategic family therapy and 'respect for persons', suggests that more plausible than the strict interpretation of 'respect for persons' would be a more liberal interpretation which requires one to treat 'respect for persons' as a desirable goal, to allow for those situations when it may be necessary to violate a person's autonomy or self-determination.

However, the example of the child at the kerbside is relatively straightforward and uncontroversial in comparison with many examples that could be taken from social work practice, in which the justification for violating someone's autonomy or right to self-determination is not so straightforward. One such case might be that of deciding whether or not to 'accept' into residential care (against her own wishes) an elderly, confused person, judged to be incapable of caring for herself adequately, and also possibly to be in some way a danger to herself. Whilst it would appear that there are sufficient grounds to argue that such a person needs to be 'looked after' in order to protect their (future) interests (as perceived by others?) and self-determination, it is harder and more complex a matter to justify this violation of the person's immediate autonomy than it is to justify pulling the child back from the kerbside.

One of the differences between the child at the kerbside and the elderly confused person is that of assessing the degree and type of danger in both cases. The danger in the child's case is obvious, definite, and the immediate violation of the child's autonomy in order to protect the 'future' person is easily justified. But in the case of the confused elderly person, whilst the dangers involved in the person remaining at home are obvious, they are not necessarily imminent, and possibly may not even be realized; the degree to which they threaten the well-being of the person needs to be assessed in terms of an estimation of the degree of risk involved, and in terms of the wishes of the person (that is, to remain at home).

In their discussion of respect for persons, Clark with Asquith comment that rights or values derivative of 'respect for persons' (such as the right of self-determination) are qualified or limited, in that they may be denied in certain circumstances. For example,

(a)   where the interests of others are adversely affected to an unacceptable degree;
(b)   where there is a persistent wilful refusal to act morally;
(c)   where the person's actions break the law;
(d)   where the person's actions will damage his interests. (1985, pp. 30–31)

However, again, these qualifications themselves raise some critical questions. For example, with respect to (a), 'the interests of others' and 'to an unacceptable degree' beg many questions about who has the power in such a situation to define 'interests', 'adversely affected' and 'unacceptable degree'.

This analysis obviously raises some important questions about 'respect for persons' as a social work value. This is especially so in the context of the expectation of it as being the paramount social work value that describes the basis of the social worker's relationship with the client. This relationship is considerably more complex than is initially suggested in a simple statement of the value or ethic.

Two areas of critical questioning emerge from the analysis so far. First, the matter of who is granted the status of 'personhood' is critical, given that many clients of social workers are people with identities that do not easily 'fit' notions of 'personhood'. Second, questions also arise regarding the extent that 'respect for persons' provides an ethical base for social work that understands and relates to the individual in their social, political and cultural contexts.

These questions will be addressed further in the final chapter of Part I. First, it is useful to examine in some detail, the equally problematical concept of self-determination, as the roots of this concept arise directly out of and are central to 'respect for persons'.

2 Client self-determination

Within social work, self-determination (self-direction) has probably received more attention than any other value. Intuitively, it is at the heart of what is generally considered to be one of the central tenets of social work:

> ... social workers should stimulate and enhance the client's capacity for making his [sic] own decisions and living his own life by his own standards. Social workers should not deceive or propel the client into a course of action that runs contrary to his true wishes. (Clark with Asquith 1985, p. 31)

It is also a value that has received much critical interest and comment, for example, McDermott (1975), Jamal (1994) and Braye and Preston-Shoot:

> Society's resources are unequally shared, and self-determination for a black elder who has no state pension, no housing rights, language barriers and is on a hospital waiting list for specialist health care will be very different from that of a retired, white self-employed owner-occupier with a private health care scheme. (1995, p. 37)

Self-determination is seen first as an ethical principle, the breach of which negates the principle of 'respect for persons'; and also as a matter of 'common sense', in that manipulative or coercive intervention is seen as not being effective in the long run. However, as was briefly indicated at the end of the last chapter, this principle or value is very difficult to understand in any absolute form.

Raymond Plant (1970, pp. 26–7) argues that social work moves away from the principle of 'respect for persons' when it begins to impose limits on, or violates client self–determination, and in so doing moves from a concept of 'negative freedom' to 'positive freedom'.

Basically, as it is characterized in most social work writing, self-determination contains these two aspects, 'negative freedom' and 'positive freedom', although, as Zofia Butrym comments, 'the paramount importance attached to the principle of self-determination in social work for most of its history is only matched by the degree of confusion regarding its nature' (Butrym 1976, p. 54). Certainly, there are many different ways in which a complex concept such as self-determination may be defined and used (for example, as seen in F.E. McDermott's 1975 collection of essays). However, as McDermott suggests (1975, p. 6) some of the confusion arises out of a failure to distinguish between the different versions of self-determination.

Negative freedom

Defined in its literal sense, which is the sense in which it is taken to be a part of 'respect for persons', self-determination refers to 'that condition which an agent's behaviour emanates from his [sic] own wishes, choices and decisions' (McDermott 1975, p. 3). In this sense, most human beings have a capacity for self-determination, and it is because of this that the term is not usually used as a description (because it does not actually add anything to a description of someone), but rather, it is generally used to 'express our commitment to it as a value'.

The most celebrated writer on the principle has been John Stuart Mill, particularly his essay 'On Liberty' (in Warnock 1962) which is a powerful defence of the right to individual freedom. Mill argues that the state, or society at large (and its appointed agents), may only interfere with the freedom of individuals if it is to prevent them from doing harm to others. On this view it is wrong to coerce or manipulate a person simply to prevent her from harming herself or to prevent her from doing something which is considered morally wrong, but does not harm others. However, Mill does make special provision for children and others not capable of making 'rational' decisions by making them exceptions to his principle.

The traditional 'negative' exposition of self-determination as a social work value very much follows the literal definition as described by McDermott above. Biestek, for example, describes the principle, as 'the practical recognition of the right and need of clients to freedom in making their own choices and decisions in the casework process' (Biestek 1974, p. 103). Biestek goes on to say that one activity which is at variance with the principle is that of manipulation, that is, the manoeuvring of the client: ' ... to choose or decide modes of action in accordance with the caseworker's judgement in such a way that the client is unaware of the process, or if he is aware of it, he feels "moved about" against his will' (1974, p. 107).

Zofia Butrym describes self-determination as a negative freedom as 're-flecting an individual's right to manage his [sic] own life and to make decisions concerning it' (1976, p. 52). Similarly, Raymond Plant (who draws on the work of Isiah Berlin, describes negative freedom as encompassing 'non-interference', 'non-manipulation' and 'freedom from constraint'. Isiah Berlin himself describes negative freedom as 'freedom from [interference]' (1969, p. 131).

The reason why this analysis of freedom is characterized in philosophical thought as a 'negative' form of the concept of freedom is that its value and meaning lie in the desire to remove the obstacles in the way of one's exercising a capacity which one has. It also demands that others should refrain from coercing or imposing their will upon one.

Ruth Wilkes goes further and defines negative freedom in a more radical way when she says: 'Negative freedom is freedom from interference, the freedom to be what I am whether anyone likes it, or approves of it, or not' (Wilkes 1981, p. 56).

The exercise of self-determination as negative freedom can be curtailed in many ways, most dramatically by imprisonment, but also by the imposi-tion of legal penalties, by threats, and by various forms of psychological pressure and control.

There is also a case referred to by McDermott (1975, p. 31) and by Ragg (in Timms 1980, pp. 222–5) for extending the concept of freedom to cover controls on individual self-determination that arise from economic and social systems in so far as these are subject to human choice and control. For example, although a person may not be physically or legally prevented from obtaining adequate nourishment for herself, she may, because of her social position, be too poor to afford it. It could be argued that such poverty is just as much a curtailment of freedom (the freedom to obtain adequate nourishment) as might be any physical or legal restrictions.

Within social work, the dominant conception of the value of client self-determination is that of its being a condition of, or a means towards the development of the client. Florence Hollis sums this up very forcibly:

> Why do we put all this stress on self-direction? Because we believe it is one of the greatest dynamics of the whole casework approach. Because we believe that the soundest growth comes from within ... for this growth from within to occur there must be freedom to make mistakes as well as to act wisely. (Hollis 1967, p. 26)

The commitment to the value of self-determination in the promotion of client development clearly indicates that the client should be accorded freedom in the negative sense of the word. However, as McDermott (1975, p. 7) points out, whether the obligation to refrain from coercing or manipulating the client should be regarded as stemming from a fundamental right of the client as a rational human being (as according to 'respect for persons'), or merely as a pragmatic or technical principle for achieving certain social work goals is the point at which controversy breaks out. Certainly, though, it is apparent from the above quotations and explanation how the concept of negative freedom fits into and is central to Kant's 'respect for persons'. It is an essential part of the view of people as rational, autonomous, self-determining (within societal limits) individuals.

However, the actual place of 'negative freedom' in social work practice is not clear, and according to many commentators is non-existent. Martin Davies sums up what seems to be a commonly held opinion about the principle of self-determination (as negative freedom) when he comments that recently, the principle has been exposed as something of a fraud: 'Both Plant and Whittington effectively killed off the concept as a prerequisite of social work two decades ago, but the idea has remained a powerful fiction in the minds of practitioners' (Davies 1994, p. 147). Similarly, Helen Harris Perlman (in McDermott 1975, p. 65) has described self-determination as 'nine-tenths illusion but one of the grand illusions'. However, the concept is not disposed of so easily, as it is still evident, albeit as a 'powerful fiction' in BASW's *Code of Ethics* (1996) which refers to the 'self-realisation of each individual person'.

Whittington (1975, pp. 81–92), lists a number of ways in which the social worker limits client self-determination:

1   Through the functions of her employing agency which might require her to use coercion or to have to employ statutory functions
2   Through the 'worker's power over clients' which stems from the worker's official (professional) power, for example, the power to decide whether or not to liaise on the client's behalf with the fuel boards when supply is threatened
3   Through the 'setting of the agency and the realities of time'. This refers to the institutional norms of the social worker's employing agency to which the social worker must conform (to a greater or lesser degree) in order not to alienate herself, which in turn might reduce her ability to do the best for her client.
4   'Pressure and high caseloads', which limit the opportunity for the social worker to give time and encouragement, if not just to recognize the client's right to self-determination.

Whittington also suggests that although the social worker may profess a commitment to client self-determination, non-directiveness and the client's right to choose, she may find her therapeutic aims greatly aided by the client's susceptibility to her 'influence and subtle directiveness'. Whittington concludes:

> To increase the client's capacity to evaluate choices may be a goal of treatment, and participation may be a technique used to this end, but to maintain that treatment is carried out without directiveness because the latter's skilled and subtle nature has made it less easy to observe, requires nothing short of self-deception (Whittington 1975, p. 91).

In his summary of the views of Whittington and Alan Keith Lucas (McDermott 1975), who also criticizes the role of self-determination in social work, McDermott makes two points regarding their arguments. First, he says that the recognition of the right is incompatible with the authority and function that social workers are required to carry out. Second, to implement the right in practice would be unworkable, which, McDermott comments, implies that in so far as social work is working now, it is because the client's right to self-determination is accorded nothing more than 'lipservice' (McDermott 1975).

Positive freedom

Zofia Butrym, in discussing self-determination, suggests that the concept has moved away from being an expression of 'negative freedom' to being an expression of 'positive freedom', which she describes as 'an extension of the range of choices available both within the personality and in the external environment' (Butrym 1976, p. 52). This move away from negative freedom has resulted in the social worker being more concerned with guiding the client towards more effective self-determination, in place of a concern for protecting the client's right to non-interference. This view is also held by McDermott, who says that 'those who identify the concept of self-determination with that of positive freedom tend to play down its status as a right, and to emphasise its role as an ideal, or end to be pursued in the casework process' (McDermott 1975, p. 7). (It is interesting to note here that this view of self-determination has a utilitarian flavour, which contrasts with the Kantian base of self-determination as a negative freedom.) Another important consequence of this view is highlighted by Ruth Wilkes: 'The idea of positive freedom is concerned with the realisation of one's true self and justifies interference in the lives of others for their own good and for the good of society'. She gives the warning: 'Coercion is usually recognised as a threat to freedom, but also intervention in the life of another for their own good may be just as inimical to individual freedom' (Wilkes 1981, p. 57).

These are important points and will be considered in more detail later on, particularly with regard to how they relate to the concept of 'respect for persons'. First, though, I will explain how and in what way it is argued that self-determination as positive freedom is justified.

Most human beings are capable of self-determination, although their capacity to exercise it rationally or constructively varies from individual to individual, and may also vary from time to time within each individual's life. From this it is possible to form an ideal of self-determination as positive freedom, on which one puts the highest possible value. Strictly speaking, this is to value self-determination not for itself (as characterized within 'respect for persons') but for the qualities, such as rationality, that characterize it in this ideal form. According to this 'idealist view', to be self-determining is to 'be liberated from the bonds of ignorance, prejudice and passion' (McDermott 1975, p. 5). It can also be seen as liberation in a socialist sense, from the crippling effects of a repressive and social system.

Of these interpretations of positive freedom, it is the idealist one that has dominated social work and so self-determination has come to be seen as something to be worked towards rather than as a basic right (the view of self-determination as negative freedom). By this view, whilst self-determination in the 'ordinary' (negative freedom) sense of the term is still considered as valuable in promoting the client's development, it tends to be subordinated to the view of self-determination as a positive freedom, which allows for the denial of the former right in the pursuit of the latter ideal.

In his essay 'Self-determination: king or citizen in the realm of values?', Saul Bernstein places self-determination (which he initially uses in its literal, 'negative freedom' interpretation) in such a context (1975, pp. 34–42). He begins by asking the question 'Just how determining should self-determination be?' in order to examine whether self-determination (as 'negative freedom') should be the paramount ('king') social work value, or whether it should be regarded as just one form of or aspect of self-determination and social work values, the use and applicability of which is dependent on the particular situation and other considerations which might affect or modify the exercise of, and the ability to be self-determining. The basis of Bernstein's argument is what he considers to be the 'supreme social work value' – 'human worth' – which he describes as 'based only moderately on what people are; much more on what they can be' (p. 40).

Legal and civil rights, standard of living, freedom to develop potentialities, and intellectual and artistic interests are all important facets of this concept: 'As we study and diagnose each situation, our concern should be for maximising the choices for the people we serve' (Bernstein 1975, p. 41). For Bernstein, the value of human worth – his supreme, or 'king', value – modifies self-determination, which whilst remaining 'supremely important' is not the supreme value: 'If what the client wants will result in the exploitation of others or the degradation of himself, the worker should try to help him change his desires' (1975, p. 40).

Bernstein discusses self-determination in stages of its complexity (self-determination 1–6), starting with self-determination 1, which is its formulation in its basic, negative freedom sense, and ending with self-determination 6, in which he describes the value of human worth and the relationship of self-determination (in its basic sense) to it. The complexities include: considerations about the dimension of time and the social worker's professional qualifications; that is, the difficulty which the social worker faces in assessing what the client wants and in helping her to achieve it, taking into account the varieties of ambivalence and changes over time. Also included are the effects of biological (health), economic and legal realities of self-determination, that is, that any exercise of self-determination which ignores such realities is 'unhealthy' and self-defeating. Closely related to this is the social dimension of self-determination: 'the complex network of social relationships which move the notion far from the simple level on which each client does what he wants to do, yields to his own impulse' (p. 37). This also involves protecting the client's legitimate self-determination where it is being violated. The complex process of decision making is also an important consideration in self-determination. For example, only as one takes account of all the relevant factors does true freedom operate in decision making: 'Yielding to unexamined impulses is more a surrender to instinctive drives than the expression of mature self-determination' (p. 39).

The discussion above indicates that the conception of self-determination as positive freedom is the one which in terms of role, aims and methods (whether 'statutorily' or 'professionally' determined) is dominant in social work. However, as was seen briefly through the quotations from Biestek and Wilkes, this conception of self-determination is open to the dangers of manipulation and coercion. Bernstein himself is aware of this when he writes that in addition to its values, the methods of social work also requires stress on self-determination (in its literal sense): 'People can be and are manipulated, but constructive changes which take root inside the person, group, or community usually need to be based on participation and consent' (Bernstein 1975, p. 41).

Referring to the bulk of social work practice as having internal change as its goal, he argues that such a change is not achieved through imposing or giving orders, but by the active involvement of the client who comes to accept, on deepening levels, the process of change. He also argues that while social workers may 'enable, stimulate, impose, or even use force', what the client feels, thinks and ultimately values is her own private affair, and more within her control than that of the social worker.

However, Bernstein's argument here is not totally convincing and is at best only partial. To simply argue that in the final analysis, the individual's 'inner life' remains, or is something which is 'private' is questionable even if it could be tested in any way. But perhaps more important, Bernstein's defence avoids any questioning of the aims, goals and methods of social work itself which the criticisms of self-determination as positive freedom point towards.

One such criticism has come from Raymond Plant, who in referring to positive freedom writes: 'Freedom conceived in this way may sanction influence and interference in a person's life if it is likely to secure the goal of that person's self-realisation in the style of life toward which he is being influenced' (Plant 1970, p. 33). As mentioned earlier, Plant's analysis leans heavily on Berlin's 1969 essay 'Two Concepts of Liberty', in which Berlin demonstrates how positive freedom evolved historically from a desire for self-mastery into a system of tyranny. Plant appears to fear a similar process within social work if the concept of self-determination is limited to 'positive freedom' and 'respect for persons' severely weakened. Plant (1970, p. 27) quotes from Hollis's statement that: 'the client's right to self-determination exists until it is demonstrated that the exercise of this right would be highly detrimental to himself and to others' (Hollis 1940, pp. 5–6). Plant argues that if self-determination is a right, as it is according to the Kantian formulation of 'respect for persons', then it is difficult to see how its exercise can in any way be dependent on the social worker's assessment of the situation (implicit in Bernstein's argument). He points out that there are groups of clients which have been regarded as being incapable of exercising the right to self-determination. For example, he cites L.C. Lane, who, referring to parents of 'difficult' children, remarks that 'the client frequently is not in a position to evaluate his [sic] problem by his own closeness to it ... the helping person is outside the problem and can therefore see it more clearly' (Lane 1952). Similarly, clients have been denied the opportunity to exercise their right to be self-determining by virtue of their 'official identity' or label, such as mentally ill or having learning difficulties, to an extent that ignores their actual abilities or 'rights'.

What concerns Plant here (and in examples from Hutchison and Perlman which he also cites) is that 'only certain things which the client chooses to do are to be counted as decisions' (Plant 1970, p. 20). When a question arises about the ability of the client to be self-determining, the social worker becomes the authority:

> ... and this kind of view could sanction casework influence or even interference in these cases where a client is supposed not to have taken a real decision according to the criteria for decision making which are given by the casework theorists. (Plant 1970, p. 29)

For Plant it is very difficult to find any sort of knowledge which could justify such criteria. Once self-determination loses its status as a 'right' and becomes an ideal or goal, there is a danger of social work theory being used to manipulate and coerce people in the name of 'freedom': 'I am claiming that I know what they truly need better than they know it themselves. What, at most this entails, is that they would not resist me if they were so rational and as wise as I am, and understood their interests as I do' (Berlin 1969, p. 133).

Another ardent critic of the performance of positive freedom in social work has been Ruth Wilkes. She describes positive freedom as 'concerned with the realization of one's true self and justifies interference in the life of others for their own good and the good of society' (1981, p. 57). Wilkes argues that intervention in another person's life can be just as great a threat to their freedom (self-determination) as coercion is recognized as being. She argues that the wish to be in charge of one's own life may lead 'high-minded persons' (social workers?) to think that they must make it as easy as possible for the individual to realize her 'true' self and master her 'bad' self. It is easy, she argues, for society/social workers to convince themselves that for the good of other people, individuals (clients) must be given insight into what they really want or really are (as opposed to what they actually want or think they are). Once this is done, knowledge of their expressed wishes is assumed and they are helped to realize their true potential by 'well known techniques of management and manipulation'. And so, the individual or client becomes her 'best or most reasonable self', and 'the empirical matter-of-fact self is strictly controlled' (Wilkes 1981, p. 57).

Very interestingly, Wilkes (1981, p. 58) provides two contrasting lists of what she sees as the distinguishing features of negative freedom and positive freedom:

NEGATIVE FREEDOM (empiricist)	POSITIVE FREEDOM (rationalist)
Main features:	
Empirical and unsystematic	Speculative and rationalistic
Spontaneous and little understood	Utopian
Inarticulate	Plausible
Assumptions:	
Essence of freedom is spontaneity and lack of coercion	Freedom is realized in attainment of a collective purpose
Method is trial and error	Method is enforcement of pattern
Cannot do good, can only avoid evil	Can make man workable

| There is an essential human nature | Human nature is mouldable |
| Man is fallible and sinful | Man is naturally intelligent and good |

We can see from the two lists that whilst Wilkes puts the argument in a wide philosophical context, she basically agrees with Plant, in that through the adoption of self-determination as positive freedom, the rights of the individual have been superseded to a great extent by the externally determined 'ideal' of the person. Whilst she accepts that social workers accept the value of the individual as an end in herself, once the emphasis is on conscious, planned change (as in self-determination as positive freedom), it is 'not possible to stand back and let things be': 'Activities are goal orientated, task-centred, and purposeful, and social work intervention, more often than not, is based on approval in terms of what is socially acceptable' (Wilkes 1981, p. 59).

Wilkes' argument goes significantly beyond Plant's criticism of positive freedom when she describes how the idea and assumptions of positive freedom have come to dominate and reflect the kind of society in which we live. The assumptions of positive freedom are, she argues, very much taken for granted, whereas the word 'negative' has come to be associated with derogatory implications in contemporary thinking, because it runs contrary to our problem-solving way of looking at the world. When the idea that the individual (client) can be improved by someone else (social workers) is linked to the idea that values are 'man-made', the result is, she says, a 'recipe for disaster': 'It is dangerous because of the absence of moral values and because of the authority it gives to experts to impose their views of others' (Wilkes 1981, p. 59). Here she is referring to a view of people based on the assumption that we create ourselves, and that there is no 'substantial self', and thus we are able to mould and control people. Human nature is essentially something which is culturally determined and open to change by human behaviour. An alternative view (which Wilkes argues for) is that human nature is a part of 'basic reality' and it does not change with different circumstances, and is essentially the same everywhere. The first concept of humankind implies that it is 'possible to discriminate between human beings by concentrating on those [or parts of ...] who are amenable to improvement by various methods' (1981, p. 61). Thus, she argues that the old, the senile, the sick, the dying, severely disabled people (all 'minimal' persons in terms of their 'personhood' status?) are a low priority because they are not amenable to change. According to the second 'world view', a person's dignity is not related to any personal attributes such as 'virtue, youth, or social value', but to that which is inherent in every person, and so 'love of one's neighbour applies to all, by virtue of one's common humanity, and no exceptions are permitted' (1981, p. 61).

Running through Wilkes' argument is the need for a morality or ethic which transcends the 'material' life of 'humankind', in the way that the Kantian 'respect for persons' is universal and a measure by which we can evaluate our goals and actions as being moral or not.

Self-determination is a problematical concept philosophically, and as is seen in the analysis above, in terms of its relationship to social work practice. The crucial issue here is the extent to which self-determination appears to be less a 'right' of the client than it legitimates intervention in the life of the client. In terms of directly protecting the client from the harm or injury, this is relatively uncontentious, but in terms of intervening in the life of the client to 'improve' their quality of life, or in terms of 'assisting' them to adapt their behaviour so that it is more acceptable to their family, to society/the community that they live in; or intervening to 'protect' society, the concept becomes increasingly questionable. Any one of these interventions may be justifiable by distinguishing between short-term and long-term interests of the client, or in terms of the social worker's duty to protect the interests of others which may be suffering because of the actions of the client. But two important questions arise, first relating to 'who' has the power to decide what is appropriate or inappropriate (what are the professional and societal processes that identify what is in/appropriate?). Second, if self-determination is more a 'gift' than a 'right' then in terms of the social worker/client relationship, where is the client's defence or protection against inappropriate or harmful social work intervention in their lives?

3 Social contexts, individualism and professional ethics

As far as their application to and use within social work is concerned, it is obvious that once one goes beyond simply stating what the values of social work are, their actual meaning is unclear and at times ambiguous, especially in the context of their role as guidelines for practice. Indeed, in the context of social work practice, from the questions and criticisms raised (for example by Whittington and Plant) it appears that the relevance of and use of these values within practice is questionable.

The aim of this final chapter in Part I is to examine some of the issues emerging from the preceding discussion and analyses of 'respect for persons' and 'self-determination'. These issues essentially address two related areas of questioning – first, the extent to which the value base of social work relates to the social context of practice and people's lives, and second, the philosophical tensions within the notions of 'respect for persons' and 'self-determination' themselves.

Individuals in context

One of the main criticisms of the Kantian 'respect for persons' as the central social work ethic is that its focus is primarily on the relationship between the social worker and the client, to the extent that this relationship is removed from the social context in which social work is practised (Corrigan and Leonard 1978; Simpkin 1979). This focus on the individual (client) potentially has three related consequences: First it hides the social context of their lives, for example, low income, unemployment, poor housing, etc. Second, it ignores possible structural inequalities and processes that create the individual's social context, and therefore play a part in causing the problems (such as low income, etc.) that the individual faces. Third, it can lead to the 'blaming' of the individual for the problems that they face, by focusing on their inability to cope with their situation, rather than seeing their problems as a result of structural inequalities in society.

A consequence of this decontextualization of the individual/client is that their identity and needs are at risk of being pathologized (a risk often realized), in that the 'problem' is seen as lying within, or 'is' the individual/client themselves. From this, it is possible to identify a close philosophical and political relationship between 'respect for persons' and the concept of 'individualism' (Horne 1995).

Steven Lukes describes individualism as:

> ... a doctrine of explanation which asserts that all attempts to explain social (or individual) phenomena are to be rejected unless they are couched wholly in terms of facts about individuals. It excludes explanations which appeal to social forces, structural features of society, institutional factors and so on. (Lukes 1973, p. 122)

As we saw in Chapter 1, BASW's *Code of Ethics* (1996) also has as its starting point, the 'individual', central to which is the relationship between the social worker and the individual. Although reference is made to the social worker's wider responsibility to 'bring to the attention of those in power, and of the general public, ways in which the activities of government, society or agencies, create or contribute to hardship and suffering or militate against their relief' (BASW 1996, para. 9), it is secondary to the focus on the individual, and is a rather weak contextualization or recognition of the import of structural factors/inequalities. It also offers no guidance as to how this relates to the social worker's other responsibilities. Both the BASW *Code of Ethics* and Lukes in his description of individualism, subordinate, if it is recognized at all, the social context of the individual. The key difference between the two lies primarily in the degree to which the individual is seen to be exclusive of her context.

With respect to social work, the significance of this can be seen through the criticism throughout the 1970s and 1980s that has been made of the use of the focus on the individual in the social work relationship. For example, Corrigan and Leonard (1978), Bailey and Brake (1975), Simpkin (1979) and Langan and Lee (1989) all criticize social work for failing to understand, account for and relate to the client in their social, economic and political contexts. Whilst not all of these critics relate their criticisms to social work's ethical roots, Simpkin (1979, pp. 97–100) identifies social work values as based on Kantian ethics as establishing ethics as impersonal principles. Respect for persons is based on the notion of the 'general human individual' (with the qualities of rationality, autonomy and personhood) and thereby separates the individual and ethical issues from the 'subjective' context of any one individual's social world or social situation. For Simpkin, this results in 'respect for persons' being understood and 'used' outside of the social context in which social work is practised.

Particularly during the 1980s and 1990s this criticism has been extended to include dimensions and experiences that relate to the identity of the individual, from feminist, anti-racist and anti-disablist perspectives, for example, Dominelli and McLeod (1989), Dominelli (1988), Ahmad (1990) and Oliver (1990). Bandana Ahmad writes:

> Fundamental to the casework model of social work is the western ideology of individualism, which perceives the individual as an entity and encourages that individual to supersede all social constraints by 'liberating the self' and 'securing individual rights'. (1990, p. 12)

She argues that as the individual is identified as the 'problem' by overlooking any relevant 'external constraints' that they may be suffering from, the social worker becomes part of a process by which 'the "problem" of the individual is personalised by the social worker to the extent of perceiving the individual as the "problem" and internalised by the client to the extent of losing any confidence of "solving the problem"'. The social worker's role is to provide 'treatment' to 'cure' the client's problem: 'Thus the client is at the receiving end of professional control, leading to an unequal exchange which perpetuates the ever increasing dependency of the client on the one hand and never decreasing control of the professional on the other' (Ahmad 1990, p. 12).

The effects of this process of 'individualizing' the problems or difficulties that the individual faces is clearly illustrated by looking at the 'social work experience' of Black clients and disabled clients.

With respect to Black communities, social work, with its origins in the Western philosophy of individualism, and the Kantian imperative of 'respect for persons' actually provides the basis of social work relationships with Black clients that at best ignores relevant cultural considerations, and at worst is explicitly racist in its approach. Azmi (1997) suggests that the concepts of 'respect', 'personhood' and 'rationality' may themselves be ethnocentric and therefore the understanding and relevance of these may not be shared or agreed by the client. Ahmad (1990) argues that most Black communities do not make clear distinctions between the individual and others:

> ... [it] is necessary to understand the problem of the individual within the roles and performances of not just the individual but the family and community

network as well … Thus the individual is not 'individualised' to the exclusion of other restraints and factors that may have either caused his or her problem or exacerbated the nature of the problems. (Ahmad 1990, p. 14)

There is also a close link between individualism and the medical models of social work in which the needs ('illness' or 'malfunctioning') of the individual are identified as the problem created by the client herself. Thus for example, the difficulties that an individual with a physical impairment might experience are seen as a problem which is a result of their impairment (which the 'properly adjusted' (!) client recognizes and accepts), rather than as a consequence of society's failure to accommodate their needs, whether in terms of disadvantaging structural features, or discriminatory social and cultural norms. Mike Oliver (1990) gives a comprehensive analysis and explanation of the ways in which Western capitalist society creates or 'constructs' disability through social, political, economic and cultural processes.

Again, individualism has been identified as one of the key factors in the pathologization of disability and disabled people, including people with learning difficulties. From a historical perspective, Oliver (1990) identifies how the development of industrialization and capitalism, required individuals to sell their labour, which necessitated a break from more collectivist notions of work and value located within the family or community. According to 'individualism', someone's value is located in them as an individual, and derived from their usefulness, that is, their contribution to wealth-creating processes. As disabled people could not meet the demands of individual wage labour, they became controlled through exclusion. This in turn led to the medicalization of disability as it is seen as an individual pathology, to be explained and 'treated' by experts or professionals solely in terms of the individual's impairment. Central to this is a questioning or denial of the 'rationality', 'autonomy' and 'personhood' of disabled people.

Webb and Mcbeath referring to Kantian ethics as used as the basis of the relationship between social workers and their clients, comment 'Adherence to the moral law is no longer a creative task of equal partners but turns towards a one-sided assertion of psycho-social mechanisms of control' (1989, p. 495).

A 'structural' agenda for social work?

From the analysis above, there is at the very least a contradiction between the 'individualist' premises on which social work is based ethically and the need for structural change in society. CCETSW (1989, 1991, 1995) has attempted to address the need to accommodate awareness of structural factors by making it necessary for social workers to develop and demonstrate an awareness of structural oppression in their training. This focus on anti-oppressive social work practice can be seen in the necessary social work values listed by CCETSW (1989), which include:

> [Qualifying social workers must be able to]:-
> - develop an awareness of the inter-relationship of the processes of structural oppression, race, class and gender;
> - understand and counteract the impact of stigma and discrimination on grounds of poverty, age, disability and sectarianism;
> - demonstrate an awareness of both individual and institutional racism and ways to combat both through anti-racist practice;
> - develop an understanding of gender issues and demonstrate anti-sexism in social work practice;
> - recognise the need for and seek to promote policies and practices which are non-discriminatory and anti-oppressive. (CCETSW 1995, p. 16)

Similarly in 1995, CCETSW identified that to achieve the Diploma in Social Work:

> ... students must demonstrate in meeting the core competencies of social work that they:
> - Identify, analyse and take action to counter discrimination, racism, disadvantage, inequality and injustice, using strategies appropriate to role and context; and
> - Practice in a manner that does not stigmatise or disadvantage either individuals, groups or communities. (CCETSW 1995, p. 4)

By contextualizing the 'traditional' values, these lists are in fact an attempt to meet some of the criticisms of the basis and use of social work values stemming from the radical, anti-racist and anti-oppressive critiques. However, there is a contradiction here in that these contextualized values are listed alongside the more traditional ones that firmly have their roots in the Kantian notion of 'respect for persons' and all the problems associated with this notion as a base ethic for social work. Commenting on this contradiction, Bill Jordan writes:

> But structural oppression requires structural change. Since power advantages are located in certain assets – wealth, whiteness, maleness – they can only be ended by redistributing these assets, or abolishing the advantages associated with them ... Liberal values, property rights, and traditional personal morality are among the strongest intellectual defences of these privileges. Yet social workers are required to uphold these same principles – rights to privacy and choice,

individual freedom and family responsibility – at the same time challenging their consequences in the forms of social injustice and discrimination. (Jordan 1991, p. 8)

The implications of this contradiction in the context of the nature of social work are discussed further in Part III. However, it is worth identifying here a further aspect of the problems associated with the Kantian base for social work's values (which Bill Jordan in the quote above alludes to), and the limitations of contextualized lists of social work values. This relates to the prevailing normative assumptions of 'who' the individual is. Charles Husband argues (1995) that contextualized lists of social work values still fail to adequately address or recognize other dimensions such as the significance of 'culture' and the part it plays in identifying as normative, different conceptions of the individual. This is an important point especially in the context of the dominant concept of the individual within British society: 'There is still the one approved way of being in British society: white, non-disabled, heterosexual, Christian and preferably male, and the different marginalized groups each have a unique relationship with this monolith' (Taylor 1993, p. 130).

This raises worrying issues regarding the role and adequacy of 'respect for persons' which as we have seen is highly questionable regarding what 'rationality', 'autonomy' and 'personhood' mean, and how they are used to construct the normative ideal of the person against whom we are measured and against which many of us may fall short. Respect for persons essentially rests on culturally specific notions of the individual that determine what the essential characteristics of the person actually are. These characteristics are not neutral or universal – they have different meanings and emphases in different cultural contexts. If different cultural and contextual aspects of the individual are not recognized, then respect for persons as the underlying ethic of social work, is potentially a further disadvantaging and oppressing factor in many people's lives in their role as clients of social work: they are measured against an 'ideal' that is itself tyrannical to their identity and experience.

Professional ethics

As there are problems regarding the denial of the social and structural contexts of the individual, there are also serious philosophical tensions regarding 'respect for persons', which add to the analysis above and help to clarify the issues as they relate to social work practice. This can be done by looking at respect for persons and self-determination as negative freedom;

and self-determination as positive freedom in the context of deontological and utilitarian ethics, respectively. Whilst both 'ethics' have initial appeal, they also suffer from serious weakness in the context of being guides for making ethical decisions, which is particularly relevant to social work.

Respect for persons (including self-determination as negative freedom) belongs to the deontological 'camp', in which certain actions are inherently right or good, or right or good as a matter of principle, and thus ought to be engaged in; as was argued by Ruth Wilkes, self-determination should be a 'right'. The problem, however, with this approach is that it fails to provide the necessary guidelines for resolving conflicts of opinion or duty which the individual may be faced with. This relates specifically to social work in that, as was mentioned in the introduction, social work is reluctant to face possible conflicts in its 'value talk', or relate its ethics to conflicts (or possible conflicts) of opinion and expectations in social work practice.

The utilitarian approach argues that actions ought to be performed, or beliefs held, not because they are intrinsically good, but because they are 'good' by virtue of their consequences. Within the context of social work, the value of self-determination as positive freedom lies not so much in its inherent worth as 'a right', but in view of the consequences or benefits of being self-determining. In other words, self-determination is instrumental to the 'ideal' functioning of the individual rather than expressive of some ultimate conviction, as it is in its negative form in respect for persons.

However, as Reamer (1982) points out, there are dangers and problems within utilitarian ethics. First, utilitarians have not yet determined how consequences that are qualitative in nature can in fact be quantified. How and by what criteria can the 'good' of self-determination be quantified? Second, they have not solved the problem that the rights of a few can be subordinated for a presumably greater good. That is, the 'rights' of an individual or individuals could be denied or manipulated to conform to the 'ideal' or greater good of others (the majority?). As was seen in the arguments of Plant and Wilkes, this is precisely what makes the advocates of negative freedom suspicious because it opens the door for manipulative or repressive actions and policies.

The distinctions between deontological and utilitarian ethics are important to consider because actions and policies implemented on these bases will often have substantially different aspects. Also they offer a means of understanding and explaining some of the apparent 'value' ambiguities within social work practice.

By asserting the value and rights of each individual person, respect for persons (and self-determination as negative freedom) is deontological in its nature. This is, however, in contrast to the utilitarian aim of promoting the common good, which Clarke with Asquith (1985) and Davies (1994), for example, suggest is the function of social work. As such, social work depends primarily on the concept of 'positive' freedom, which expands the area of what can be considered to be 'justifiable paternalism'. According to this view, the function of social work is seen as an activity which promotes the resources and opportunities considered necessary for a decent or 'good life', and which involves taking a wide range of welfare responsibilities, 'even when the intended beneficiaries have not sought help' (Clarke with Asquith 1985, p. 62). To have a need implies lacking a 'good' whose possession is, in an important way conducive to happiness (or acceptability). From this, the task of social work can be seen as an attempt to maximize the well-being of individuals and that of the community as a whole.

Clarke with Asquith comment that, 'social work is not merely a service to be provided in a neutral or passive manner for those who choose to make use of the kind of help it can offer' (1985, p. 62). Not only is social work not neutral or passive, but many commentators (see above section) identify social work as serving a function in society that aims to control certain individuals or groups in order to serve the interests of more powerful groups. In the light of this, the utilitarian base of social work at best offers no moral protection to, and may actually further disadvantage or oppress, people with marginalized identities. At worst it may provide justification for the 'control' of certain people for the 'good' of 'society'. Either way the role and function of the social worker is problematical.

Brief though this analysis is at this stage, it does offer a means of understanding the nature of some of the 'value' problems and conflicts within social work. The social worker essentially is caught between a deontologically based set of 'professional' ethics, and a utilitarian-based practice 'reality'. In local authority social work, the agency has a responsibility to ('the good') society as well as the individual, and the social worker employed in the agency therefore has a responsibility to represent society's interests, expectations and ideals, as well as the 'rights' of the individual. In this context, social work's code of ethics does not appear to offer the social worker any clear resolution of the moral issues that arise out of this situation of potentially conflicting demands. Statements such as: 'Members of a profession have obligations to their clients, to their employers, to each other, to colleagues in other disciplines, and to society' (BASW 1996) offer no guidance to the social worker precisely at the point where dilemmas specific to social work practice arise.

Related to this criticism, and also offering an explanation of the failure of social work values to relate to social work practice, is Pearson's argument that:

... while the social work ethic gives a more elaborate account of client *rights*, it gives only the poorest indication of the other side of the equation, (i.e. that client rights are limited): the social worker's ethic in theory offer a limitless relationship, although in practice, of course, the social worker is able to offer no such thing. For the social worker is an official of a bureaucratic organisation, as well as a person engaged in a 'relationship'. (Pearson 1975b, pp. 50–51)

Two important points emerge at this stage. First, traditionally, 'value talk' in social work tends to concentrate solely on the relationship between the social worker and client. Second, social work, as suggested in the previous argument, is practised within (local authority) organizations, the demands of which necessarily affect the way in which social work values 'work'. Pearson illustrates this by listing two sets of values. First he gives a 'traditional' list of values (1975b, p. 50), and then he gives a 'hidden' list of values which takes account of the organizations/bureaucracy in which most social workers are employed, and the 'realities' of social work practice. According to the 'traditional' list:

1   The client has a right to expect that his [sic] communications should have a confidential status.
2   The client has the right to determine the course of his own actions [the principle of self-determination].
3   The client has the right not to be judged by the social worker [the 'non-judgemental' attitude].
4   The client should be regarded with warmth and positive feelings, whatever his actions [the notion of 'acceptance'].
5   Underlying all these is a general principle of 'individuation', each man is unique; all men have innate dignity and worth. (Pearson 1975b, p. 50)

However, according to the 'hidden' list:

1   The client's communications to officials of a public service, involving as they do matters of public money, and in the last analysis public order, have the character of public knowledge.
2   The client's actions, impinging on the rights of others and on the obligations and priorities of public service, are not free.
3   The client's actions, by their nature problematic to 'consensus', are judged.
4   The client's rights as a citizen do not entitle him to anticipate that regardless of any act on his part he will continue to be 'accepted': he can, in short, be 'outlawed'.
5   Clients, as the objects of a large-scale organisation with many bureaucratic features, will be treated within an administrative machinery as 'cyphers'. (Pearson 1975b, p. 53)

The ambiguities, compromises and obvious infringements of the 'traditional' list, Pearson argues, cannot be simply dismissed as bad social work practice. They represent society's, and the social work agency's, demands and expectations of the social worker, and the 'bureaucratic' nature of the agency: 'if social work is anything, it is an organisationally grounded practice, and social work's ethic is but one side of an incomplete equation' (Pearson 1975b, p. 51).

It is a failing of much that has been written on and about social work values that it has concentrated solely on the relationship between the social worker and individual client. Where reference is made to the context in which this relationship takes place, it is mostly secondary to the relationship itself and offers no more than a vague or general reference which avoids examination of possible conflicts of values. The references in Part I to BASW, CCETSW and the argument from Downie and Telfer illustrate this point.

Yet from the discussions above of the significance of the social context of people's lives, of deontological and utilitarian moralities and Pearson's argument, it seems obvious that in order to examine and understand what social work values are, and how they 'work' in practice, the context in which they are practised must be given equal consideration. That such things as societal and structural aspects, expectations and norms, agency demands and functions are important in understanding social work values has been demonstrated in this chapter. The actual role and function of social work's value base is at the very least problematical, raising a number of important questions and issues.

In order to examine these issues further and in greater detail it is useful to look specifically at what happens to values in actual social work practice, which is the aim of Part II of this book.

Part II

Values in practice

Part II furthers the analysis of social work values begun in Part I by examining what happens to social work values in social work practice. This is done by closely examining two case studies (Chapters 4 and 5), each of which raises important issues that both illustrate some of the main points emerging from Part I, and also contribute further important questions regarding social work values and the nature of social work. The two case studies relate respectively to an elderly person, Mrs M and a young mother, Sheila with a three-month-old child at the time of referral. Both case studies raise a number of issues relating specifically to the notions of 'respect for persons' and 'client self-determination', in the context of two key areas of contemporary social work policy and practice: community care and child protection.

In both the first edition and for this second edition of *Values in Social Work*, I engaged in a number of interviews with practising social workers who described to me cases that they were involved with, or had recently been involved with. It is from these interviews that the case studies are derived.

The aim of the interviews was to find out and examine how social work values (concentrating on 'respect for persons' and 'client self-determination') 'work' in social work practice. In particular, I was interested in the extent to which social work values in the relationship between social worker and client are affected, compromised or determined by 'outside' factors such as agency function, and expectations from other professionals, groups or individuals. Added to this, I was also concerned with understanding the wider processes by which the individuals (clients) came to the notice of the social work agencies and social workers concerned in the first place.

The interviews were conducted with individual local authority social workers who described a particular case that they were currently involved with, or had been involved with very recently. This was to avoid general statements about what values social workers thought were or were not important or relevant, and also to avoid simply compiling a general list of considerations or constraints regarding values in practice. By basing the study on specific current or very recent cases, it was hoped to be able to identify and examine in detail how social work values actually (rather than 'might' or 'should') work in practice.

The interviewees were asked to relate the 'story' of the case, that is, describe the sequence of events, and the nature of their involvement, from which I concentrated on what I considered to be the important events and decisions in the light of value issues and decisions made. I did not impose any structure or predetermined set of questions on the interviewees, but did have a set of general 'headings' or 'clues' to which reference could be made during the interviews. These were:

- Assumptions   Whose? Why
- Presumptions   What? Whose?
- Decisions   What? Whose? Who with? Why?
- Standards   Whose?
- Whose values?   Social worker's
  Social work agencies'
  Other professionals'
  Client's
  Society's
- What was the social worker's role/task?

This list of 'clues' was intended to focus my listening and questioning of the cases to enable me to identify what values were relevant to the case, and how they were working.

It would be illegitimate to draw any conclusive or 'universally applicable' conclusions about how social work values operate in specific types of cases from the two case studies. However, I think that the cases are *illustrative* in a general sense of the way in which values are affected and determined in practice by other considerations/factors, and, specific to the cases described in detail, illustrate in depth social work values at work.

Obviously in the descriptions and analysis of the cases, the names of the people involved have been changed to protect their confidentiality, and the social worker in each case is simply referred to as 'SW', although it should be remembered that the social worker in each case is different. In the descriptions of the cases themselves I have, as far as possible, used quotations from the social workers in order to give as full and accurate a description as possible of how they described their cases to me.

The first case presented, Mrs M, is included from the first edition of *Values in Social Work*, as it remains a very powerful illustration of a number of pertinent issues relating to respect for persons and the client's right (?) to self-determination, in the context of current community care policy and practice. The second case is the result of a new interview and is included for the complex issues it illustrates around 'respect for persons' and 'client self-determination' in the context of concerns around child abuse and child protection. Both case studies also raise questions about 'who' the client actually is.

4 Mrs M – description and analysis

Description

This first case concerns Mrs M, aged 94 years, who lived on her own in a rather neglected, large detached house. She has a son (who works in Saudi Arabia), and two daughters, Mary and Maureen. Mary has recently had cancer and visits her mother occasionally (but regularly), and Maureen visits twice a week, sometimes more. Mrs M was first referred to the local social services department by her daughter Maureen, who said that her mother was finding it increasingly difficult to look after herself properly, despite her (Maureen's) regular visits. She also said that 'the job was getting her down and she never received any thanks or acknowledgement from her mother for the things that she did for her.'

A social worker (SW), visited Mrs M, finding the house to be 'smelly and tatty', and described Mrs M as 'a forthright and domineering old lady,' and she 'refused to accept any help from us. She told me all the help she wanted was someone to do up her buttons because she had severe arthritis'. Her arthritis meant that Mrs M was often unable to dress herself properly, and that she frequently dropped things. SW also described Mrs M as having poor eyesight and as being forgetful, for example, she would turn on the gas and forget to light it:

> She was also smelling and it was fairly obvious, although she would never let me go look in her bedroom, that she was probably sleeping in a wet bed and wet sheets, except for when her daughter [Maureen] came round and actually changed the bed for her.

Following SW's visit, the home help organizer visited Mrs M (on the suggestion of SW) and her help was also refused. Over the next year SW visited several times a week to

> ... maintain contact ... with my style of social work, when I go see somebody like Mrs M, and they resist offers of help, I don't simply close their case and go away until the inevitable crisis occurs. I feel it's important if possible to form a relationship with them of some sort so that eventually when they do have to move, they are not totally alone, but that they have got some sort of warmth and someone that they can trust.

However, Mrs M still refused any help, and the case was closed:

> We were getting nowhere, and then we reopened [the case] when her daughter [Maureen] again asked for help. It was the same reasons: that the daughter was saying that she couldn't go on with the level of help that was needed, and she was getting so little reward from her mother for all that she was doing ... The pressure was beginning to tell on her and she in fact was going to the doctor with a bad back which was probably due to the tension and strain of it all.

Soon after, Mrs M accepted a home help and the incontinent laundry services were started, 'so the situation had got pretty bad'. Following this 'the daughter found the situation improved and the case was then made non-active'. Some months later Maureen again visited SW and said that she and Mary were going to try and persuade their mother to accept permanent residential care in the new year. SW visited Mrs M in the new year and found that her situation had deteriorated:

> Mrs M's faculties are fading, and it seems to me that she is at risk. I felt very much that Mrs M could no longer cope living alone, and I talked to her about considering some sort of change, so that I was quite keen for her to go for some short-term care so that she could get some idea of what a residential home was like ... often she would get up at 6 a.m. and light the fire before the home help got there, and she would sit very close to the fire, and she would put things like wet knickers to dry very close to the fire, so that it was a danger. I was also very aware that she was not feeding herself properly. She would talk to me about having quite nutritious meals, but when I discussed it with the home help, you could see from her wastebin that she was probably living on bread and butter and hot drinks, and her 'Sanatogen' – her favourite tipple.

SW persuaded Mrs M to visit a private residential home for the elderly with her and also a local authority-run home, and although Mrs M said that she liked the local authority home, she stoutly refused to go there as a resident, even for a 'short break'.

At the end of February, the daughter Mary told SW that both she and Maureen were getting fed up and she felt that they would not be able to cope much longer. Maureen was now seeing her doctor 'for her nerves'. SW went to see the GP (who was Mrs M's and her daughters' GP), and they agreed that she (SW) would try to persuade Mrs M to go into the local authority-run home (which Mrs M had previously visited and liked), while Maureen went on holiday. Mrs M agreed to go to the home for two weeks over Easter, and it was arranged by SW that the home could provide a permanent bed for her should 'there by any chance that she might agree to stay there'. However, a few hours after her admission (at which she seemed quite happy), SW had a phone call from the home saying that 'Mrs M was creating mayhem and they couldn't cope with her any longer, so please would I take her home?' SW went to the home and tried to reason with Mrs M but was unsuccessful: 'She said that if I didn't take her home, she'd hail a lorry. She's 94 don't forget.'

So Mrs M returned home and SW arranged extra home help visits over the Easter holidays while Maureen was away. Immediately after the Easter holiday, SW received a letter from Mary saying that she was not going to visit any more – 'she just couldn't go on any longer with it'.

Meanwhile Mrs M was behaving very obstructively towards the home help, refusing to let her change her bed and on one occasion she 'raised her walking stick to her':

> When the GP talked to her about her selfishness she said she wanted to change her GP. At this point we discussed the possibility of a Section 47 [of the 1948 National Assistance Act], but agreed that there were not yet grounds for this. But if the family stayed clear as they were saying they would, the situation would soon come to it.

On SW's next visit, she found Mrs M to be 'happy as a sandboy', looking forward to the return of Maureen from holiday. However, despite the extra home help hours that Mrs M had been receiving, she described her 'condition' as deteriorating:

> There were faeces on the floor and the bed was wet every night ... she always sat in the same chair, and that was very well awash. She has an open fire in her oak-panelled sitting room where she sat all the time, and there was a considerable risk with this I thought.

Between May and July, the situation remained much the same. An attempt was made by SW to get Mrs M to go for day care in the hope that this would lessen some of the pressure on her daughters, mainly Maureen, and also provide practical support for Mrs M during the day. Mrs M tried it for two days but then refused to go any more. At the end of June, Maureen had a 'violent argument with her mother and told SW that she would no longer continue to visit her mother'.

At the beginning of July, SW received a letter from the home help organizer saying that Mrs M was leaving the gas on unlit, and that she was claiming that the home helps had stolen spoons, forks and silver from the house. During a later investigation of blocked drains it was found that Mrs M had flushed the missing items down the toilet. SW also received a letter from the Gas Board expressing concern at the risk of the gas being left on, and saying that they felt that the gas should be disconnected. Once again, SW and the GP considered using Section 47 of the National Assistance Act 1948 after the Gas Board's threat to disconnect, but once again decided that they did not have sufficient grounds to do so (this is discussed in further detail later on). Mrs M's was becoming 'a very complex case of somebody who in many ways is becoming senile, but is extremely cleverly manipulating the situation'.

On SW's next visit, Mrs M agreed to accept Meals on Wheels, but the day after they had started SW received a note from the Meals on Wheels organizer saying that Mrs M had told them not to call again. At about this time Mrs M began telephoning her son-in-law at work, up to a dozen times a day, which was 'causing him considerable difficulties at work … She usually rang to ask him to do things for her such as replace her kettle, which she regularly burnt out by switching it on without putting any water in it.'

At the end of July, Mrs M became ill with a urinary infection for which her GP prescribed a course of antibiotics which, he suspected, she was not taking. At the end of August, she made further allegations that her spoons and silver were being taken: 'I found it impossible to reason with her.'

At the same time British Telecom contacted SW to inform her that they were going to charge Mrs M each time they had to reconnect her telephone. Apparently when she could not get through to someone she was ringing, she became angry and 'pulled the wire out of the wall'. She also started to complain to the police that her daughters were refusing to visit her: 'If she wanted to stir things up with the family she'd say that nobody had been near her.'

In September, Mrs M spoke to SW about 'going into a home for the winter', and SW took her to visit a privately run home, which she said she would be willing to go into in December. But unknown to SW, she had advertised in the local paper 'a room to let for a student', which contradicted her intention to accept residential accommodation. Mrs M did not 'let' a room and refused to discuss going into residential accommodation.

At the beginning of October, SW received a note from the home help saying that she had had to climb into the house through an open window on her last visit because Mrs M could not get the door unlocked. By now there was no contact at all between Mrs M and her daughter Maureen:

> Mrs M would say things to me like, 'the daughter's a devil', and 'I never want to see her again.' In fact the daughter was extremely upset and said that by visiting her mother she was only making herself ill and was not helping the situation at all. I agreed with her.

Two days later:

> ... things came to a head because when the home help arrived there was a strong smell of gas and the home help found that Mrs M had jammed the gas tap full on, and she tried to stop the home help phoning for help, and insisted on returning to the kitchen to light the gas. The home help had to forcibly remove the matches from her, and the home help phoned the office. By this time Mrs M had found more matches and wanted to go back to the kitchen, but 'they' got the Gas Board out and the home help got Mrs M to the garden, with difficulty. The Gas Board arrived and cut off the gas, so Mrs M had no means of cooking. [She was also still refusing to have Meals on Wheels.] On the following day I had a meeting at the house with the community physician and the GP. Mrs M had, the previous night, attempted to heat up water in a saucepan on the open fire, and on the visit with the community physician and the GP, she agreed to go into our home at ... where there was the only vacancy.

In explaining why it was at this time that the community physician was involved, SW commented: 'I felt that the point was reached when she could no longer manage on her own, and in the circumstances there was no other help we could give her to enable her to stay at home'. Both the community physician and the GP agreed that Mrs M could not remain at home.

> ... and the community physician who is always extremely reluctant, thank goodness, to make orders, said that in his opinion an order would be granted, but if there was any chance she would go 'in' voluntarily, we should try that first. But if she went in to the home and did as she had done previously, and demanded to be taken home again, then he would invoke the order. So it was that near, and the GP absolutely agreed with this.

'On the one hand I will support somebody's right to independence to the hilt, but ... '

I would now like to look in greater detail at the role played by SW, by illustrating from the interview how her relationship with Mrs M (and the subsequent action taken) developed, and the extent to which it was influenced by the interest and concern of Mrs M's family, SW's consideration of the community in which Mrs M lived, her GP, and the adequacy of the domiciliary/community-based services that she received. I will also illustrate what SW's own thoughts and feelings were during her involvement in the case.

Family

Consideration of Mrs M's family was (increasingly as the case progressed) an important factor in SW's intervention in the life of Mrs M. The initial and second referrals both came from Mrs M's daughter, Maureen. Also, as the case progressed, both daughters complained to SW of the mental and physical strain that they were under in caring for their mother. This pressure from the family increased as Mrs M's faculties decreased and also as Maureen and Mary's relationship with their mother deteriorated, to the point eventually where contact between them and their mother ceased altogether. The family's practical support of their mother also became an important consideration in whether or not Mrs M was able to, or should remain at home: 'we [SW and the GP] discussed the possibility of a Section 47, but agreed that there were not yet grounds for this, but if the family stayed clear, the situation would soon come to it.'

SW was sympathetic to the plight of Maureen and Mary, and her consideration of their plight played a significant part in her decision to:

1   Persuade Mrs M to accept domiciliary support;
2   Attempt to persuade Mrs M to accept short-term care whilst Maureen went on holiday;
3   Persuade and eventually force Mrs M to accept permanent residential care, which originally was the family's decision.

In explaining her reasoning and motives behind these decisions and her eventual considerations about the applicability of Section 47 of the National Assistance Act 1948, SW said:

> Yes, there's various factors. There's the family who were extremely upset, and the daughter who stopped visiting was on the verge of a breakdown about the whole thing – it had really got her down. I was obviously very aware of the anguish of her family and that must have come into my reasoning.

A small, but specific, example of SW's awareness of, and receptivity to the 'family's anguish' can be seen in the quotation below. I asked SW whether she had considered any alternative means of cooking when the Gas Board first expressed concern in July:

> No, we talked this over with the family – what about getting her an electric cooker? They begged me not to consider an electric cooker. She had had electric cookers in the past and simply either turned them on and left them on, or turned the plates on until they were red hot, and then put the tea towels to dry on them. The risk was just as great – it seemed to me that there was no alternative.

Neighbours and community

Another important consideration for SW in the case were the interests of Mrs M's neighbours and local community:

> She was also a great nuisance to the neighbours. She was forever ringing and asking them to do things for her, and she was also using the 'Good Neighbour Scheme' beyond what was reasonable. She would ask them to take her into the city to buy some tea and then be unable to get into the shop to do it ...

When I asked how important her demands on and her relationship with her neighbours were in assessing Mrs M's 'fitness' to remain in the community, SW replied:

> I think it is important, because she lives in a village where there's a fairly high proportion of elderly people in the village who get good support from the 'Good Neighbour Scheme', and as I said earlier they have a caring GP who visits his elderly patients frequently, and no pressure is put on these people to give up their homes. I felt that Mrs M had gone beyond the point where she could be cared for by the village, and by the social services within the community – it was residential care or nothing ... I felt that she had reached the end of the community caring that was available.

The GP and domiciliary service

SW described Mrs M's GP as excellent: 'he is one of those paternal type GPs, and he visited her six weekly':

> We would have a monthly meeting at the surgery between the GPs, the Health Visitor and myself, the social worker, and she [Mrs M] would have been discussed at every surgery meeting, usually on the lines of 'what are we going to do about Mrs M?', and he [the GP] saying that there's no way she can go on looking after herself, and me saying well, we haven't yet got grounds to force her to do anything.

On several occasions SW and the GP discussed the possibility of getting a psychiatrist to do a domiciliary assessment, but:

> Each time we came to the conclusion that there was no point in getting a psychiatrist to do a domiciliary visit. And even on the day when the community physician came out, he felt the same ... he felt there was no psychiatrist who would section this lady ... I know that it is extremely difficult to convince a psychiatrist doing a domiciliary visit with a client like this, who is as articulate as Mrs M, that she is senile to the point that she needs to be admitted to a home because she is a danger to herself and others.

The home help organizer also expressed concern over Mrs M, particularly from the Easter period when the home help's hours were increased while Maureen was on holiday, and from July after the home help had first smelt gas in the house:

> The home help organizer felt she could not put in more hours for Mrs M, and there was certainly pressure from that direction for me to try to get Mrs M into a home, because she had a lot of help for a long time, and was still deteriorating, and that aspect came into it as well [the justification of persuading Mrs M to accept residential accommodation].

The home help organizer's opinion was that, relative to the resources at her disposal, she felt that she could not provide adequate care for Mrs M. There was also the problem of Mrs M's sometimes belligerent and uncooperative behaviour towards the home help to be taken into account.

SW's perspective

I think that it can be seen from the description and illustrations above of SW's relationship with Mrs M's family, her GP, the domiciliary service involved, and her consideration of the community of which Mrs M was a member, that there was considerable pressure on her to 'do something about' Mrs M. I will discuss this in more detail in the next section. First, I think it is important to mention another form of pressure that SW felt herself to be under, which is illustrated by the following:

> On the one hand I will support somebody's right to independence to the hilt, but I often picture the headline – 94-YEAR-OLD LADY LIVING ALONE, FALLS INTO FIRE, WHAT DID SOCIAL WORKERS DO ABOUT IT?' ... I was aware that she would make a classic case of this sort of treatment in the newspapers. I would often have the 1948 Act open before me to see if she might meet the criteria ... so I found it a very, very difficult case to work with.

This anxiety or fear felt by the social worker was in fact 'very real' when understood against the background that in recent months social workers had been castigated in the tabloid press following the death of two elderly people living alone, who were 'known' to their local authority social services departments.

The first part of this quotation, 'On the one hand I will support somebody's right to independence to the hilt, but ... ' accurately summarizes the nature of the difficult role and task that SW had in this case. In the place of her fear of doing nothing and the 'worst' happening and it being scandalized by the press, one could easily change the quotation to: 'I will support somebody's right to independence to the hilt but ... one must consider the cost (emotional and physical) to her family ...' or: 'but ... one must consider the high concentration of domiciliary services (but still inadequate) that she was receiving ... ' or: 'but ... her family, her GP, the home help organizer, her neighbours all thought that her behaviour and demands had exceeded what could be accommodated in the community, and therefore she should be "persuaded" to go into a home'.

Analysis

The client's right to self-determination and Mrs M

The crucial area of interest which I shall examine in this case is Mrs M's right to be self-determining, 'reflecting an individual's right to manage his own life and to make decisions concerning it' (Butrym 1976, p. 52); or as Ruth Wilkes has put it, 'freedom from interference, the freedom to be what I am whether anyone likes it, or approves of it or not' (Wilkes 1981, p. 56). The immediate implication of this is that Mrs M has the right to live her life according to her own wishes, the respect of which should be the social worker's responsibility.

However, almost throughout the whole case, this right of Mrs M to be self-determining was under threat, and was eventually denied her altogether. Although, technically speaking, Mrs M eventually accepted residential care 'voluntarily' (that is Section 47 of the National Assistance Act 1948 was not invoked), she was not free to choose whether or not she wanted to go into residential care. If she had refused, the Act would have been invoked straight away, and so in effect her 'right' to remain at home was taken away from her despite her expressed wish over the months to remain there. It would therefore appear that other criteria relating to her life were eventually deemed to be more important than her right to 'manage her own

life'. That is, the effect of her management of her life on herself, but principally, it seems from the interview with SW, on other people (family, community, 'caring services') was judged (by all concerned), to be beyond what
was acceptable or tolerable by society's standards and expectations.

So in the context of this case, the value of client self-determination as a
right is not a value that exists solely in the context of the relationship
between the social worker and the client. Rather, Mrs M's right to self-
determination existed also (and perhaps increasingly so), in the context of
her relationship with her family, neighbours, local community, her GP, and
the demands she was making on the domiciliary services (although these
demands were made more on her behalf to meet her needs as perceived by
others, rather than her needs as perceived by herself). There were four
main, and interrelated considerations that affected Mrs M's right to self-
determination.

First, there was the consideration of, and assessment of Mrs M herself by
SW, her GP, home help organizer, and in the end, the Gas Board. As the case
progressed, this assessment of Mrs M moved towards the opinion that Mrs
M was not capable of looking after herself 'adequately' at home. There was
also an element of risk to herself and others (though undefined by everyone
except the Gas Board) from a gas explosion or fire. From the GP's point of
view, there was general concern about her health (severe arthritis and a
urinary infection), and from SW's and the domiciliary services' perspective
there was concern about her ability to look after herself adequately or
safely. This concern developed to the point at which it was discussed between SW and the GP as to whether the conditions necessary for invoking
Section 47 of the National Assistance Act 1948 might be present. The Act
provided the guidelines and justification for denying Mrs M's right to self-
determination, although it was agreed that until the Gas Board disconnected her gas supply, there were not sufficient grounds to invoke the Act,
despite everyone's concern.

Second, SW took into account Mrs M's relationship with her two daughters, and the demands that she was making on her neighbours and local
community. With regard to her family, the emotional and physical strain on
them was an important consideration, particularly from the point at which
they said that they could no longer lend practical support to their mother,
which had been a major support to her remaining at home. With regard to
Mrs M's neighbours and the local community, SW felt that Mrs M's behaviour, her dependency, and the risk she presented eventually surpassed what
she felt the local community could or should support.

Third, SW had to consider the adequacy of the support available and
given to Mrs M in the community through the social services department in
the light of her deteriorating health and increasing need for services (need

that was defined more by the social services than by Mrs M herself). Mrs M's willingness or not to accept available support was also a consideration. Account had to be taken of the home help organizer's view that Mrs M required more home help hours than it was possible to give her. From this, one could argue that a client's right to self-determination in cases similar to Mrs M is also affected by or dependent on an assessment of the domiciliary support required by the client and whether limited resources are sufficient to meet the degree of support required. This is an important consideration when examining community care policies and practice.

Fourth, SW had to consider the wishes and demands of other individuals or agencies concerned. Importantly, both the GP and the home help organizer expressed the opinion that Mrs M was no longer capable of continuing to live in the community. Pressure also came from Mrs M's family for her to go into a 'home'; whilst not having the same 'weight' as the GP's opinion that Mrs M was not really fit to remain at home, or the home help organizer's declaration that it was not possible to give Mrs M the extra home help hours that she needed, the family's wish was important, if only because of the amount of practical support that they gave to their mother, and which was eventually withdrawn.

As the case progressed, Mrs M's right to self-determination was evaluated in the context of all of these considerations, whose importance increased as Mrs M's mental confusion and physical health appeared to deteriorate, and she was judged to be in need of more and more support. It is, however, interesting to note that a psychiatric assessment of Mrs M was never done, although it is not clear from the interview with SW whether this is because it was decided it would have been totally inappropriate, or because there was little likelihood of it providing the necessary grounds for 'removing' Mrs M, against her will, to residential accommodation. What is clear is that Mrs M's right to self-determination decreases as the concern and demands for 'something to be done' about her increase. The client's right to self-determination appears in this case to be principally a right that may be superseded by consideration of the interests and demands of 'society', which themselves may be in conflict with those of the individual client.

The social worker's role

In the light of the denial of Mrs M's right to self-determination, I would now like to examine more specifically the role played by SW. As we have seen in Part I, according to much of the social work literature and theory on values, the social worker's relationship with the client derives from the Kantian imperative of respect for persons, in which the individual's right to self-determination is of central importance. However, as we have seen here, SW was also receptive to the needs and demands of 'society', to the network of family/community relationships in which Mrs M lived, which were in conflict with the wishes and the ability of Mrs M to live her life as she wished, without interference.

This conflict also exists (and remains unresolved) within professional 'values' statements, for example, CCETSW '[Social work students must] promote people's rights to choice, privacy, confidentiality and protection, while recognising and addressing the complexities of competing rights and demands' (1995, p. 4).

But this could, and in the case of Mrs M does, clash with respecting a person as a self-determining individual, if recognition of 'competing rights and demands' is seen as legitimizing or compromising the individual's rights. This apparent confusion or contradiction in the social worker's responsibilities is very well highlighted by the case of Mrs M, in which SW's role appears to be based as much on her concern and responsibility to society (including Mrs M's family, local community, the 'health' and 'caring' services), as it was on her concern and responsibility for Mrs M and her wishes, certainly as expressed by Mrs M herself.

However, it would be a mistake to view the way Mrs M's right to self-determination diminished simply in terms of a compromise or denial of her rights. If we consider the notion of self-determination in its 'positive freedom' interpretation, then intervention in Mrs M's life can be ethically justified on the grounds that it prevents immediate harm coming to her, and potentially protects her long-term interests. We also need to consider that central to SW's role in her consideration and assessment of Mrs M was her statutory responsibilities as a local authority-employed social worker.

This responsibility is expressed and formalized by Section 47 of the National Assistance Act 1948, and Section 1 of the National Assistance (Amendment) Act 1951, which as long as the grounds specified in Section 47(1) are satisfied is now more commonly used as it gives authority 'in the interests of that person to remove him without delay'.

Section 47(1) of the 1948 Act states that:

(1)   The following provisions of this section shall have effects for the purposes of securing the necessary care and attention of persons who:
   a)   are suffering from grave chronic disease or, being aged, infirm or physically incapacitated, are living an insanitary conditions, and
   b)   are unable to devote to themselves, and are not receiving from other persons, proper care and attention. (quoted in Norman 1980, p. 79)

Specifically, the Act represents SW's statutory responsibilities, and in a more general sense, represents SW's responsibility to society. This responsibility and concern was apparent in the case from the time of the first referral and SW's initial assessment of Mrs M and provided a continual source of reference.

It is interesting to note, however, that in this case, the Act's interpretation by SW appears to have served more to protect Mrs M's right to self-determination, up until the point when her gas supply was finally disconnected, than it readily provided the grounds for sooner denying her that right. SW remarks in the interview that during her regular meetings with the GP and the health visitor, the GP would argue that Mrs M could no longer continue to look after herself, to which SW would reply that they did not have the grounds to force her to do anything. This remained the situation until the family stopped supporting their mother, and the gas supply was disconnected.

Nevertheless, SW's statutory responsibility, and the pressure from 'society' to 'do something about' Mrs M which increased in intensity as Mrs M's faculties and acceptability decreased, provided the focal point to the relationship between SW and Mrs M.

Essentially, SW's role in the case was one of mediation, that is, she had the task and the problem of balancing her responsibility to 'society', the statutory requirements of her employing agency, with the wishes of the client. The value of the client's right to self-determination has to be seen within this context, which clearly sets limits upon it. SW was necessarily, as part of her job, a party to, and a central figure in assessing and defining these limits to Mrs M's right to self-determination.

To begin with, during the case, she was able to allay the 'need' to deny Mrs M's right to self-determination by persuading her to accept domiciliary support. SW's role here can be seen as mediating or negotiating a compromise between Mrs M and 'society'. That is, she was able to meet the right of Mrs M to stay at home and also, on behalf of society, assist Mrs M to live at what it considered to be an acceptable standard. However, as the case progressed, SW became more responsive to the concern and demands of Mrs M's family and the other 'health' and 'caring' workers involved with Mrs M and the relationship between Mrs M and the local community. Fairly quickly, as Mrs M's needs (as perceived by others), and the strain she put on her family and community increases, she moves closer to the state that reaches the limit of what 'society' can accept or tolerate, and SW's focus of concern moves more to representing 'society' than representing the wishes and rights of Mrs M.

With respect to Mrs M's right to self-determination, it is not simply a case of it being compromised by the social worker; it is more a case that Mrs M's right was limited to begin with, and SW's job was to represent the concern and demands of society as much as it was to represent the interests and rights of Mrs M. In this case, society's values and expectations outweighed the client's right to self-determination and it was a part of SW's role/task to represent and be instrumental in implementing those values and expectations.

5 Sheila and David – description and analysis

Description

This second case concerns a young mother and her 18-month-old son:

> The initial referral we got in terms of the case was back at the end of last year from a Health Visitor who expressed concerns about a young couple [mother, Sheila, 19 years and father, Peter, 23 years old] who had a newborn child, David – something in the region of just over three months old, and there were a number of concerns about the couple and their ability to bring up this child.
>
> In the first three months, David had suffered from oral thrush. He also had an eye infection, and a very sore bottom. These in themselves might not be major child protection concerns but the fact was that this baby was over three months old and as yet had not been registered with a GP – so the parents were not seeking appropriate medical advice for the baby.
>
> The Health Visitor expressed concerns about possible aerosol abuse by this couple because she noticed empty canisters under the sofa of this house. There were concerns about level of hygiene and cleanliness in the house – ash and cigarettes thrown across the floor; they didn't have proper feeding equipment – equipment to clean the bottles after feeds.

Following this referral SW made a number of unsuccessful attempts to make contact with the couple:

> ... we had great difficulty in getting to see the couple. When we visited, the couple either wouldn't answer the door or weren't in – we think it was the former actually. When we did eventually get in the couple did acknowledge that they were having difficulties and experiencing problems in bringing up this baby and perhaps they did need some support from social services.

The next step for us was actually to get the Family Centre involved to help them with aspects of parenting and perhaps look towards encouraging them to develop appropriate parenting techniques – seek appropriate medical advice for the child, etc. We pursued this with the couple. We then left it with the Health Visitor and she got the child registered with the GP.

We arranged planning meetings where we invited the couple and staff from the Family Centre – in order to discuss what work was going to be undertaken with them – and I think the whole area here was although there were concerns about the child which were verging on child protection, the idea was let's work with the family in ways that were productive – in partnership – offering them support and assistance. Very much in the spirit of the Children Act [1989] – it was about let's try and work in partnership with this couple and develop their parenting techniques. Lots of young people do struggle as parents – with the demands and expectations of bringing up a baby.

There were three separate occasions when we arranged planning meetings. On the first one it was at the Family Centre and the couple didn't turn up. So on the second occasion we arranged it at the family home – there was no response.

Shortly after this last unsuccessful attempt to arrange a meeting with David's parents, Sheila, the mother, made contact with the social work office to request financial help:

The parents then indicated that they had not received any letters from ourselves – which possibly may be true but ... We arranged another planning meeting and again the parents failed to show up – so it got to the stage where there were quite a lot of concerns but it was hoped that once we got the family engaged it would be a relatively low-key piece of work.

Soon after this Sheila contacted SW to say that because of the violence she was being subjected to by David's father, she had left him, and she and David were now living with a member of his extended family:

Then, as well as the other concerns, there was the housing issues as well. We managed to speak to Mum. She said that she felt a lot better now and acknowledged that there was aerosol abuse going on, but that this was being done by the child's father – by inhaling, and that she'd been exposed to violence from him. She acknowledged having difficulty caring for the child but the person that she was living with at the time was offering her a lot of support and advice, because that person had children of her own.

Obviously the housing issue remained; we agreed that some of our concerns had subsided. David's father was no longer on the scene. Mum apportioned a lot of the blame onto him – he had refused to let her leave the flat, therefore she couldn't seek appropriate medical advice for the child – and that because of his aerosol abuse he was aggressive and violent towards her. Things were a lot better now as long as she was getting the appropriate support from his extended family. We felt that we should pursue a housing needs assessment ... but when we arranged meetings Mum was either out or had left the child with the people she was staying with [his extended family].

A short time later, on one of the Health Visitor's visits to the household, the woman whose house it was, expressed concerns over Sheila's relationship with, and ability to look after David, saying that Sheila had slapped David's bottom when he would not stop crying, and on another occasion had put a cushion over his face, again because he would not stop crying:

When we spoke to Mum, she denied she'd put a cushion over his face, but did admit to slapping the child's bottom. She also said that she was having to wander about in the streets at two and three o'clock in the morning, pushing the baby around in the pram, trying to get him to sleep. She was quite annoyed that we were still wanting to be involved with her, having supposed that since she had left her partner, we would withdraw – she wasn't happy at all.

Sheila and David then left to stay with another member of David's father's extended family:

She said that she felt it was too rigid where she had been staying before – too many rules and boundaries – she couldn't leave the child there and go out and do what she wanted. We were still concerned that she was very resistant to our involvement. Also we weren't happy with where she was staying. The family she was staying with were renowned for having young people from the estate coming to stay for short periods if they'd fallen out with their parents. There was no stability there.

We were still running around trying to catch up with her in many ways – she still wasn't keeping appointments. During this time we were encouraging her to liaise with the Housing Department – we said that we would do our bit in terms of supporting her application, but she needed to make the initial application to say she was homeless. She was saying she was doing this but she wasn't. With hindsight I think she was actually fearful of getting her own tenancy knowing that she couldn't actually cope and that she would struggle – she was frightened of being on her own.

It was a case of saying to this mother that 'on this day at this time a car will be coming here and picking you up, taking you to the Housing Department to get registered as homeless so that we can start the ball rolling with helping get your accommodation, because we're not satisfied with you living here, or about moving from house to house.'

She also had a brief period with another friend – in all, three temporary addresses within the space of about six weeks.

We were trying to work in partnership, but with this young parent it felt an impossible task. So we set it all up so all she had to do was step into the car and then step back out [to the Housing Department and the Family Centre].

The Health Visitor at this time was having similar problems in maintaining contact with Sheila and David. Either they were not in when she called, there would be no response, or she would be told by neighbours that she had moved house:

> The Health Visitor was quite anxious, which is evident from the amount of correspondence she sent us: 'I visited on this day, and these were my concerns ...' Despite our involvement and repeated advising how to take her child to the doctors, she was failing to do this – on the occasions that we did have contact with Mum and David it was noticeable that either he'd have a sticky eye or he sounded chesty or he had a cold – there always seemed to be a number of minor illnesses [David was now approaching six months old].

The Health Visitor did manage to see David before the Family Centre meetings, whereupon it was found that his weight was in fact dropping:

> This mother is struggling to cope financially – she's not buying the child appropriate food and he's not being fed when he should be fed. This was reinforced at a Family Centre planning meeting [attended by SW, the Health Visitor, the Family Centre worker, Sheila and David]. The baby was initially quite happy, but towards the end of the meeting, after half to three-quarters of an hour he was quite unsettled – it was quite obvious that the child was hungry. The workers from the Family Centre said that the child was extremely hungry and gave him a bottle of milk at the meeting, which he polished off.
>
> Mum spoke a little during the course of the meeting but not to any great extent – there was always the possibility that she was going to explode/have a go at us. She perceived us as giving her a hard time. She said and had said previously you're not doing anything to help me – 'other social workers help their clients' – that kind of thing.
>
> We decided that if she came to us, which she did from time to time making financial requests, we wouldn't give her any money; instead we 'would go out and buy the food/nappies for you and will bring them to you'.
>
> We decided that the baby would be weighed weekly, to monitor his weight to make sure it wasn't dropping any further. It was also decided we would buy some baby food, feeding equipment and give it to Mum so she had no excuse for this child not being fed properly [under the auspices of Section 17 of The Children Act 1989].
>
> We still wanted the child to stay at home – we still wanted Mum to care for him – and we still wanted to work with Mother. So it was a case of alleviating the immediate crisis concerns we have about the child, but we still need to engage this mother with some meaningful work.
>
> We also got a full paediatric medical done on the baby especially because of concerns about weight being dropped; we felt we needed to seek appropriate medical advice.

By now Sheila was living back at her mother's house:

> Considering the concerns we had about Mum and the state of her accommodation, we weren't sure which were the greater concerns in all honesty – the fact that she had moved back with Mum in a filthy house and unacceptable conditions for a child to be brought up in – or accepting this – it was emerging that we thought she was really going to struggle to cope on her own if she got a place on her own, just go under.
>
> It was a case of what was the most acceptable – we weren't happy, but it was agreed in the interim the situation at her Mum's would be reasonably stable if the baby started crying. If she was having problems with the baby, especially if the baby started crying – when she had previously struggled the most – at least she had her mother to turn to in terms of support and her brothers and sisters were around as well.

Sheila's mother was also pregnant, expecting her ninth child. Her children were already on the child protection register and there were already court proceedings to put these children (six plus the unborn child) under either care orders or supervision orders, on the grounds of neglect – very poor home conditions, Mum's inability to provide any stability/home routines/boundaries:

> A lot of the way that Sheila was behaving towards her baby – her inability to do certain things, or her lack of knowledge in aspects of parenting, routine, stability, managing her finances, seeking appropriate medical advice – were still evident in her mother, and now these concerns were being identified in this young parent. She'd obviously had her mother as a role model and was doing a lot of what her mother had been doing.

Shortly after moving into her mother's house Sheila was offered a flat:

> Sheila signed the tenancy for, but she never actually moved into, the flat. She got the keys – we said we'd support her through a community care grant application to get some furnishings. She already had some from her previous flat shared with her partner. We wanted her living on her own so we could get the Family Centre properly involved in looking at her parenting. We hoped that once she moved into this flat we would be able to begin some meaningful work with her – a thorough assessment of her parenting skills and working with her on 'good enough' parenting.
>
> Unfortunately despite getting the tenancy she never got round to moving in – and shortly afterwards, I think within a couple of weeks the flat was broken into and the central heating boiler was stolen. She decided that she couldn't go live in a flat that had been broken into, but that was more about the fact that she was frightened – that she didn't feel able to live and cope on her own. We did raise

this with her but all she said while she was living at these temporary addresses was that once she got a flat of her own, 'It'll just be me and David and then we'll be able to get some peace and quiet.' So all that she'd said earlier was about getting her own place and some semblance of normality, yet when the opportunity came to get her own place she never took it up. It was about her own lack of self-confidence and insecurities and her fear of not being able to cope on her own.

In all honesty hers was a very real fear as it would be for any 18-year-old, let alone one who's not had the most stable secure upbringing herself, who really was struggling to cope; in terms of managing financially, she was fairly clueless and irresponsible.

At this stage we had no choice but to take it to case conference and bring my concerns out into the child protection arena – then that would be arguing for the child to be put on the 'at risk' register, because we felt that Mum was not coping. The concerns, when we discussed them with my line manager and co-worker, it wasn't the scale of concern it would have been if the child had been injured – a huge bruise or something like that or that the child had been sexually abused; there was lots of little concerns, a whole package of concerns, I think, that covered all aspects of parenting. It was all the stuff about not seeking appropriate medical advice, despite being repeatedly advised to do so; it was about not budgeting properly and not managing her finances. It was about the child not being fed properly; it was about the child not being clothed adequately despite the fact that we'd provided clothing, it was about this child's level of cleanliness and hygiene. Although on occasions the child would be turned out quite well, but if you actually looked closely at him, like between his toenails, it was obvious that he hadn't been bathed for some time, or hadn't been bathed properly – sore bottoms and all that were down to levels of hygiene as well, including in the house and levels of stability and security she was able to offer the baby.

On the positive side she had a good bond with her baby – and she did care for and love her baby, so there were positives there, but on the whole there were so many shortcomings in terms of her ability to actually bring up this child. So we felt we needed to go to case conference and send this case across for long-term work. We felt she was of an age, young enough to take on board advice and perhaps change, but we felt it needed fairly extensive social work involvement.

It was taken to case conference and the child's name was put on the 'at risk' register under the categories of neglect and also physical abuse on account that Mum had actually hit the baby. She admitted hitting or slapping his bottom; she denied putting the cushion over his face, but the conference felt that this was not something that it could ignore. So the child was put on the register, and if Mum wasn't cooperating at a later stage, then we'd need to be looking at instituting proceedings.

One of the recommendations of the conference was that we send mother and child to a unit for young parents where they could perhaps undertake a thorough assessment of her parenting techniques and where she would have some support available.

The case conference

It was not possible to ignore the very real concerns concerning David:

I went through the report with Mum prior to the case conference – and there were a whole range of concerns that I identified and the only thing that she eventually commented when I read the report ... was 'I don't like the way you describe my mum's house as being in a filthy state.' I did actually say that 'In the report there is a lot of stuff actually about yourself – how do you feel about that?', but she didn't say anything. She sat through the case conference and hardly said a word.

I realized at the time just how oppressive a case conference can be: the chairperson and the Minute taker were both from tl : child protection unit, there was the paediatrician who'd given the child a medical around the time the weight was dropping; the Health Visitor, workers from the Family Centre, myself and the co-worker, a legal representative from my legal section, plus a 19-year-old mother, and she'd actually brought her baby with her. That was about her wanting to prove to the conference that she could actually look after the baby, and the baby was reasonably well turned out as well.

When I look back on it, it's not surprising – a 19-year-old single parent who's had a fairly damaged childhood, very low esteem, lacking in self-confidence, very insecure and here in a room full of professionals in a quite intimidating and hostile environment for her. I had an interesting discussion with the co-worker afterwards about how oppressive case conferences can be ... how perhaps unreasonable and unrealistic we were being in expecting parents to make significant contributions to case conferences about their view of a report, what they think.

Sheila had said that there would be one person coming with her, however the person didn't turn up.

I do think that partnership with clients in child protection is a bit of a myth. I'm not sure you can work in partnership, particularly when you consider the power imbalance in terms of you're the professional with the authority – particularly in this situation ... It was clear from the onset that my relationship was going to be fairly difficult ... We had great difficulty in engaging her meaningfully, of getting her to open up and talk.

At the case conference, at the confidential stage, we decided that we wanted to send her to a residential facility where we could get an assessment of her parenting and her own needs and support for her ... but one of the things the consultant paediatrician said was that he wasn't convinced that at 19 anybody was capable of change: this kind of stuff needed to be happening when they were younger, and not when they were 19. He was quite cynical about her chances of succeeding in terms of changing, which we felt was perhaps not appropriate because we felt we needed to give her the opportunity to understand why certain aspects of what she was doing weren't acceptable. To suggest people aren't capable of change – we didn't think it was fair on her, so we said that we would pursue this package of support ...

I don't think you can be scathing or cynical, or that should be any reason not to pursue it – you can say that I think the chances of her succeeding are minimal, but I don't accept the argument that for those sorts of reasons it shouldn't be pursued. The thing that as social workers we do tend to forget is just how difficult change actually is – for anybody really, not just for people we are working with ... to some extent we're asking this person to undo the last 19 years of her life ... to become this 'good enough parent'.

Analysis

The Social Services, of course, always have a thankless task. If they are over-cautious and take children away from their families they are pilloried for doing so, if they do not take such action and do not take a child away from its family and something terrible happens to the child, then likewise they are pilloried; so it is a very difficult position they find themselves in. (Mr Justice Hollis, quoted in the *Cleveland Report*, Secretary of State for Social Services, 1988).

This statement from Mr Justice Hollis very clearly summarizes the complex nature of social work in the context of child protection. Whilst in the case described here, there is no serious suggestion that 'something terrible' might happen, the social worker and other professionals involved in the case were none the less in a 'difficult position' regarding correctly assessing and judging the welfare of David in the context of his relationship with his mother, Sheila, and her wish and 'right' to care ('adequately' in the eyes of the social worker) for him. This constantly demanded of the professionals involved, principally the social worker (SW), the balancing of the rights of Sheila, and of David, within the context of assuring his safety and welfare. This raises a number of 'value' questions that relate specifically to the notions of 'respect for persons', and 'self-determination': 'A case like this was not clear-cut – it's very much values-based, it's very much about what you see as acceptable levels of hygiene and cleanliness, about aspects of parenting. It's very value laden' (SW).

In order to examine this in more detail it is useful first to look briefly at the nature of child protection social work in the context of society's expectations, and then relate this to how the values of 'respect for persons', the 'rule of optimism' and 'self-determination' 'worked' in this particular case.

Social work and child protection

In the United Kingdom, the family is seen as the primary 'care' environment in which children are cared for, nurtured and socialized. The family is also considered to be essentially 'private', and the privacy of the family is seen to be indicative of what is meant by a 'free society'. Within this context the social work role in intervening in family life should not undermine the autonomy of the family, except where the family is clearly identified as having 'failed' in the socialization and nurturing of their children (Dingwall 1986). From this we can see that social work intervention in the family encapsulates a tension between the privacy and autonomy of the family and the responsibility of the state, through social work services, to protect the well-being of children where necessary. The social work role in the family is then a complex one, that is rooted not only by society's concern for the protection of children, but also acknowledges the privacy of, and primary socializing role of the family. This potentially creates a difficult dilemma regarding the extent to which social work can monitor or 'police' the family. This complexity and tension was highlighted during child abuse inquiries during the 1980s, particularly those concerning Jasmine Beckford and the Cleveland inquiry (see Horne, in The Violence against Children Study Group (1990) for a detailed discussion of these two inquiries).

In many ways these two inquiries gave social workers conflicting messages. The report of the inquiry into the death of Jasmine Beckford (London Borough of Brent 1985) was very critical of the social workers involved in the case for not doing enough to protect Jasmine, and found that social work in general as not using the powers available through the legal framework of child care legislation to protect children. In contrast to this, the *Cleveland Report* (Secretary of State for Social Services 1988) was very critical of the social workers involved on the grounds that the removal of a number of children was unwarranted. The two inquiries in turn, were critical for the 'under-reaction' on the part of child protection services in one individual case, and critical of services for their 'over-reaction' in a large number of cases of 'diagnosed' child sexual abuse.

The Children Act 1989 was designed in part as a response to the criticisms of child care social work in the 1980s. The foundations of the Act rest on the presumption that children are best brought up by their own families, and that families should be provided with support to enable them to stay together. Local authorities have a general duty under section 17(1):

a) to safeguard and promote the welfare of children within their area who are in need; and
b) so far as is consistent with that duty, to promote the upbringing of such children by their families.

Implicit within these principles is the notion of 'partnership' between statutory agencies and parents.

Against this background, SW's role and task in working with Sheila and David was quite complex, as can be seen above in the account of her involvement. This complexity constantly raised difficult questions as the case developed – it became apparent that 'working in partnership' was problematical, which itself added to concerns about David's safety and welfare. The assessment of the 'risk' in the situation of David remaining with his mother was a constant tension for SW:

> ... when you're working in the child protection field you're always looking at risks and levels of risk – you're working out what you perceive to be an acceptable level of risk, and that raises issues about thresholds of risks – and people have different thresholds, different professional workers as well as different teams ...
>
> Neglect is a real 'biggy' at the moment, as there is so much discussion as what are acceptable levels. When you walk into a situation of what constitutes neglect and what doesn't, my judgement may not be the same as other people's – so it is very much value-laden. There are no hard and fast rules in the majority of cases that are referred to us. It's really quite difficult – you can't exactly have a ticklist. You've got to weigh up the positives ... (SW)

Respect for persons, self-determination and the rule of optimism

The difficult area of assessment of risk relates closely both to the legal framework of SW's work with Sheila and David and the way in which the primary social work values of respect for persons and client self-determination informed SW's role and relationship with Sheila and David.

It is obvious from SW's description of the case that the value of 'respect' was central to her relationship with Sheila and David, in that SW was concerned to respect Sheila's 'right' to care for David that is, to be self-determining. This is also underpinned by the presumption that children are best cared for by their parent(s).

However, Sheila's 'right' to be self-determining is not tenable in any 'absolute' form because of concerns for the safety and welfare of David. If Sheila's exercise of her 'right' to act as she saw fit significantly compromised David's safety and welfare, then SW had an obligation to intervene to protect the safety and welfare of David. In other words, concern for David's welfare may conflict with and take priority over Sheila's 'right' to be self-determining. This obligation and responsibility has a basis in 'respect' for David (as a person in his own right) and in the statutory responsibilities of SW.

In a case such as this, both Sheila and David together are 'the client' as the family, but also Sheila and David in their own right are the clients, particularly David with respect to concerns about his welfare.

As the case progressed, the concerns for David's welfare, although fluc-
tuating to some extent, depending on where Sheila was living, generally
increased. These concerns centred around the difficulty in contacting and
working 'meaningfully' with Sheila, her housing problem, her numerous
changes of address, all of which carried concerns for David's welfare. There
were also growing concerns about Sheila's ability to care for David in terms
of her parenting skills: seeking appropriate medical advice, hygiene, nutri-
tion, and her emotional relationship with David, regarding the reported
instances of her putting a cushion over his face, and her admitting to hitting
him.

Whilst initially SW saw the client in this case as the family (Sheila and
David), as the case progressed, questions and concerns emerged regarding
David's welfare that prompted greater involvement with the family (Sheila)
in order to monitor and safeguard David's welfare. In this sense, while still
trying to maintain a relationship based on 'partnership', SW's primary
focus was on David and his welfare.

In the context of the concerns that SW and the health visitor had, Sheila's
self-determination was not a 'right' in the sense of 'negative freedom' –
'reflecting an individual's right to manage his [sic] own life and to take
decisions concerning it' (Butrym 1976, p. 52). More accurately, self-determination in this case reflected its meaning in the context of 'positive freedom':
'[Self-determination] conceived in this way [as positive freedom] may sanction influence and interference in a person's life if it is likely to secure the
goal of that person's self-realisation in the style of life which he [sic] is
being influenced' (Plant, 1970, p. 33). According to SW:

> In terms of self-determination, you're thinking where child protection is con-
> cerned, it's very difficult because if you allow the client the right to be self-
> determining, what are we saying when we come across unacceptable levels of
> parenting? On one level it was all about her [Sheila's] involvement with us – she
> doesn't have any choice in that matter and there is a point where she either
> cooperates with us or she risks losing her child.

Concern for David's welfare was sufficient to sanction interference in Sheila's
life, with the aim of supporting her in caring appropriately for David. As
the case progressed, it was realized that for this support to be effective,
more direction or control was needed, resulting in the case conference and
its decision to place David on the 'at risk' register, and the recommendation
to find a place for Sheila and David at the young parent's unit. Society's
expectations (both general and as identified specifically through the Children Act) are very well summed up by Clarke with Asquith, when they
comment that: 'Social workers perhaps sense that in a way they are ex-

pected to be on both sides of the self-determination – social control, and self-determination – paternalism boundaries at the same time' (1985, p. 40).

The value of 'respect for persons' is closely related to the notion of the 'rule of optimism' in social work, which has been the subject of much discussion with respect to child protection work (London Borough of Brent 1985; Dingwall et al. 1983; Parton 1986; Horne 1990) and which is relevant to the case discussed here.

The role of the 'rule of optimism' was given prominence by Dingwall et al. (1983). They described the concept as interpreting the behaviour of parent(s) in the most favourable way possible. That it is closely related to 'respect for persons' can be seen in the following quotation from Zofia Butrym (1976) as she describes respect for persons as referring to 'the inherent worth of man [sic]', that is, a belief in the essential goodness, and potential for 'good' in human nature. This is also expressed in the BASW's (1996) formulation of respect for persons: 'basic to the profession of social work is the recognition of the value and dignity of every human being.'

This optimism is strongly evident in SW's attitude towards, and relationship with Sheila, and is reflective of social work's value-base and the legislative framework that SW was working within. Interestingly, it also contrasts markedly with the attitude of the consultant paediatrician, in the case conference, who doubted that Sheila was capable of change, of learning to be a 'good' parent:

> Another thing about our work [social work] is that we need to hang on to the premise that people are able to change ... but I do think we sometimes are unrealistic about what changes we expect from clients – particularly when you consider they may still be living in the same difficult environment, relationships, and with the same difficult financial circumstances. (SW)

In conclusion, at this stage of the analysis, the values of respect for persons and client self-determination, whilst being central to SW's role and relationship with Sheila and David, operate in a quite complex way. They are not 'absolute' in any sense, but are to a large extent contingent, in terms of what they mean, on other factors such as the legislative framework pertaining, and the 'acceptability' or 'adequacy' of the client's (Sheila's) behaviour, attitudes and relationship with David. It isn't that the values are compromised by the social worker, or the social work process, so much as it is that they were limited to start with.

6 'I will respect somebody's right to independence to the hilt, but ... '

Members of a profession have obligations to their clients, to their employers, to each other, to colleagues in other disciplines and to society. (BASW 1996)

The two quotes above – the first one, that comprises the title of this chapter, from the social worker involved with Mrs M, and the second from BASW – indicate something of the realities of social work practice, and perhaps also the limitations and complexities of social work. This chapter begins an examination of these limitations and complexities by drawing together some of the threads or main points that emerge from the case studies presented in the previous two chapters, focusing on what happened to the values of 'respect for persons' and 'client self-determination' in practice. This examination is then developed in Part III, by looking more explicitly at the relationship between social work and society.

Whilst the case studies cannot be taken to be in any way conclusive, they do illustrate something of the complexities of values in social work. Concentrating on the two cases described in detail, the obligations of the social worker to the client, employers, to their colleagues in other disciplines, and to society, all played crucial parts (but different in both cases) in determining what happened to the social work values involved, and in our understanding of what happened. Five main points emerge from the cases of Mrs M, and Sheila and David.

First, the social work values of 'respect for persons' and 'client self-determination' were significant aspects of the relationships between the social workers involved in the two cases and their clients. In the case of Mrs M, SW, whilst having concerns about Mrs M's ability to care for herself, initially accepted her 'right' to live her own life as she wished, and to refuse the help that SW was able to offer her. In the case of Sheila and David, again whilst having concerns about Sheila's circumstances, and David's welfare, SW initially accepted a supportive, but monitoring role as Sheila attempted to sort out her problems. This is not necessarily to suggest that in either case this reflects an acknowledgement of the client's 'rights' to non-interference, that is, self-determination as negative freedom. Perhaps more accurately it reflects the lower level of concerns about each case in their initial stages; and initial optimism that in each case the clients would accept the assessments of their needs and cooperate with the support offered to them.

Second, precisely how 'respect for persons' and 'client self-determination' work in practice depends on a number of factors – neither are absolute in the sense that they unequivocally inform the nature of the outcome of social work intervention. Both are limited by the context of the particular case, including the concerns and interventions of other agents.

It appears from the two case examples that the way in which social work values function and are used is determined not solely by the social workers' relationship with and responsibilities to the client, but also by their obligations to other people, organizations and society, according to the extent that these 'other' agents are interested in, concerned, or affected by the interests and actions of the client. In both cases, 'respect for persons' and the client's right to self-determination were contingent in their use and applicability to the particular context of the case, in this sense. For example, in the case of Mrs M, her 'right' to self-determination was determined, and in the end limited by SW's obligations to her statutory responsibilities, and her consideration of and obligations to represent the interests, concerns and needs of Mrs M's GP, family, community and the adequacy of the available domiciliary services. All of these concerns and obligations were formalized through SW's employing agency's expectations of her. Similarly, in the case concerning Sheila and David, Sheila's 'right' to be self-determining was seen by SW in the context of her statutory responsibilities, including her concerns for David's welfare, and the concerns expressed by the health visitor and consultant paediatrician.

In both cases, concerns for the clients increased over time, which increasingly brought into question the client's 'rights' and/or abilities to be self-determining in their chosen goals or lifestyles. As seen in the case examples, this might involve the social worker ostensibly acting against the expressed wishes of the client, that is, Mrs M and Sheila, where their actions may be judged to harm or potentially harm the interests and the welfare of others.

Third, and closely related to the second point, it is a part of the social worker's role and responsibilities in both cases to represent the concerns and interests of others. This is particularly obvious in the context of local authority-based social work, in which the social worker has statutory responsibilities, for example, in the case of Sheila and David. In neither case was the social worker in any straightforward sense an advocate for and on behalf of the client. In both cases, the social worker had a responsibility to make judgements as to what was in the best interests of all parties concerned, which reflected points of view and wishes other than those of Mrs M or Sheila. This does of course beg important questions, particularly evident for example in the case of Mrs M about 'who' the client actually was at particular points during the case, and perhaps 'who' and/or what was the problem? 'Respect for persons', and 'client self-determination' (negative and positive freedom) exist and are used in this context.

Fourth, and again closely related to the point above, a part of the social work role in both cases is one of mediation between the client and their wishes, and the concerns and interests of others ('society'), although the exact nature, expectations and outcomes of this role were different in both cases. The values of respect for persons and client self-determination operated within this context. They did not exist either in consideration or effect, independent or 'above' this context in the sense of giving a positive ethical instruction as to what the social work role or task and relationship with the client should be.

In the case of Mrs M, we saw the considerable extent of society's interest in her (from her GP, domiciliary services, social work agency concern, neighbours, community and family) in terms of concern for her welfare and health, prompted by the effects of her behaviour, and the risks and demands that she presented to others (family, community, social services, etc.). This eventually outweighed her wish and 'right' to live her life as she wished. SW's initial task was to support Mrs M in the community, if possible (according to society's standards and expectations), which in effect meant that Mrs M's right to be self-determining was questioned and limited right at the outset. As her 'condition' was perceived to grow worse, concern was heightened to the extent that her 'right' to independence was eventually taken away. At this point, SW was basically representing society's concern to Mrs M, although initially at least, she had recognized and represented Mrs M's right to be self-determining, to society, to her family, and to her GP, who had questioned Mrs M's right to be self-determining quite early on. Eventually, through this process of mediation, SW came more to represent the concern and wishes of society as its concern and demands increased in response to Mrs M's perceived 'risk' to herself and others, and the increasing demands (as perceived by the carers) she was placing on the 'caring' services.

In the case of Sheila and David, the social worker's mediation role was particularly evident in the case conference – when SW expressed 'optimism' about Sheila's ability to become a 'good enough' parent to David, given the right environment and support – against the less positive assessment and opinion of the paediatrician. In the case conference, which Sheila experienced as 'intimidating and hostile', an important part of SW's role was one of representing Sheila and her perspective, mediating between the different opinions and assessments of Sheila expressed during the meeting.

Fifth, both cases illustrate in different ways how values are used instrumentally, in which the dominant ethic is utilitarian rather than deontological. This was the case regarding Mrs M, in which her right to self-determination (as negative freedom, based on the Kantian 'respect for persons') was limited by a utilitarian ethic in which a consideration of and for the greater 'good' of the community/society, justified the denial of the individual's right to be self-determining. In the case of Mrs M, one could argue that SW was acting on behalf of the state by implementing paternalistic legislation which required her to constrain Mrs M's freedom in what was purportedly her own, as well as society's best interests. This owes more to the concept of self-determination as positive freedom and is thus based on a utilitarian rather than a deontological ethic. Similarly, Sheila's 'right' to be self-determining was dependent on her demonstrating her ability to care adequately for David.

In both cases the concept of self-determination was essentially understood and used in its 'positive freedom' understanding – thereby legitimating social work involvement in the lives of Mrs M and Sheila, with respect to protecting their welfare and interests, and the interest and welfare of others.

What clearly emerges from the case studies is that in order to begin to understand values in practice one has to examine the nature of the social work role and task. It is inadequate simply to conclude that 'professional values' may sometimes be compromised or superseded by other considerations, because this ignores the important relationship between society and the social worker. Certainly the case studies presented here suggest that this is of central importance in defining and understanding the relationship between the social worker and the client, and the place of social work values within this relationship. Therefore, in order to understand social work values in practice, it is necessary to examine the nature of this relationship between society and the social worker, which is the purpose of Part III.

Part III

Values in context

The analysis so far has raised a number of key points and questions regarding the nature and use of social work values.

In Part I, through the examination of the concepts of 'respect for persons' and 'self-determination', a number of issues were raised regarding the application and efficacy of these key values when applied to social work practice. Two main concerns that emerged from this examination related to the potential role of 'respect for persons' in underpinning the 'pathologizing' of individuals, of offering an understanding and recognition of individuals that does not recognize the social and political structures and limitations in which they live, which themselves may be significant in defining their lives and problems that they face. This raises some difficult issues regarding the efficacy of 'respect for persons' as the basic ethic in social work.

The examination of the concept of client 'self-determination' also raised difficult issues, as it emerged that within social work, the use of 'self-determination', rather than protecting the individual from social work intervention into their lives (self-determination as 'negative' freedom), is actually more likely to be used (self-determination as 'positive' freedom) in such a way that 'legitimizes' intervention on the grounds of protecting or furthering the individual's interests, or the interests of others where they may be adversely affected by the individual.

In Part II, this analysis was further developed by focusing on two case studies taken from practice, which themselves illustrated some of the complexities of social work values in practice. Conflicting interests and priorities, that may result in the denial of the individual's 'right' to be 'self-determining' emerged in both cases. In both cases, the social workers involved at some stage were representing the interests – statutory, other people's (professional and non-professional), where needs or expectations conflicted with those of the initial client. In this sense, the social workers were involved in mediating between different sets of interests and obligations. This is not simply a case of social work values being compromised in practice, but reflects interests and obligations that the social worker may have, other than those to the client themselves.

In order to examine these complexities further, Part III looks in more depth at the relationship between social work and society, and seeks to understand social work values in this context. This is done by explicitly examining the relationship between social work and society, followed by looking at the role of social work within this relationship. Finally in this section, the nature of social work's value-base is examined in the context of this analysis.

7 Social work and society

The state isn't some abstract thing, the state is the social worker knocking on someone's door. (Jordan 1984, p. 13)

Everyday social work characteristically remains a series of transactions between deprived people who have lost control over parts of their lives, and social workers with limited resources but awesome powers to coerce. (Jordan 1990, p. 164)

The 'social' in social work

In the *Concise Oxford Dictionary* and the Collins *New English Dictionary*, the word 'social' is defined as 'concerned with the mutual relations of human beings', and 'affecting public interest'. If these definitions are applied to 'social' work, then one has an activity which affects, or is in the public interest. However, as it is, this is an unsatisfactory definition of social work in that it could include many activities which would not normally be considered to be social work, such as 'middle classes running jumble sales ... scoutmasters taking difficult boys up mountains', and in a more professional sense, it could be used to describe the work of 'health visitors or GPs talking about money problems' (Anderson 1982, p. 9). These activities are all 'social', and although they refer to the general area in which social workers work, as well as the medium through which they work, they do not specify or clarify what 'social' means in the context of social work.

If one turns to BASW for clarification, they offer the following definition:

The purposeful and ethical application of personal skills in interpersonal relationships directed towards enhancing the personal and social functioning of an

71

individual, family, group or neighbourhood, which necessarily involves using evidence obtained from practice to help create a social environment conducive to the well-being of all. (BASW 1977, p. 19)

Whilst this 'pocket definition' may read well, on reflection, it could apply to many kinds of 'social' activities. Rather than starting with a description of the activity itself, in order to find out what social work is, it is more useful to relate it to, and put it in the context of the society in which we live and from which it derives its existence.

Two features common to all societies are that there are 'norms which are basic to all societies which enable people to relate to each other' (Fowler 1975, p. 90) and the recognition of some varying degree of responsibility (between different cultures) for those of its members in need. British society is no exception to this, and has organized various services provided by the community which express this sense of obligation to its members that it defines and accepts as being in need. Titmuss describes this process as 'manifestations first of society's will to survive as an organic whole' (1958, p. 39). How society identifies and defines those people that it identifies as being in need is itself interesting, and will be discussed later.

Around areas of communal interest – for example, the maintenance of social order, child-rearing practices, and care of older and disabled people – social institutions establish themselves. Some of these directly assume 'communal responsibility' and operate on behalf of society through the establishment of state agencies. Local authority social services departments are an example of one such agency, whose task it is to take an interest in certain kinds of behaviour and the social conditions of recognized individuals within society. Within this, the social work task and its objectives reflect societal norms, for example, certain standards about bringing up children. Social work then, is basically normative and social workers, as well as teachers and psychiatrists, for example, are 'socialising agents' (Fowler 1975, p. 91).

Anderson (1982) identifies the social work task as dealing with people who are in conflict with some norms in society, as a feature which separates the 'social' in social work from more general forms of 'social' work. He argues that 'the essence of the social work task is the resolution of that conflict' (1982, p. 10). If there is not a conflict of norms, then social work is not being done, although one may be working socially.

Howe (1979, p. 32) also argues that the 'social' in social work should be understood by taking it to refer to the socially sanctioned nature of social work. That is, society sanctions certain members or agents (social workers) to take an interest in the conditions and behaviour of some of its members (clients). This interest or intervention may be at the request of the client who acknowledges the interest and expertise of the social worker as appropriate to the resolution of her problem; or it may be because of a request from others, as in the case of probation.

In a similar vein, Fowler describes social work as

> … best seen as a continuum having, at the one end, help mobilised out of a sense of caring and recognition of responsibility to the individual in need, and at the other end, help which is mobilised because of the perceived threat to the established order, characterised by the criminal, mentally ill, unemployed etc. (1975, p. 89)

Such is the case where the individual (client) is defined as rejecting or being in conflict with some generally accepted norm of behaviour. It is interesting here to briefly consider from an historical perspective how and why certain identities came to be identified as potentially posing a 'threat to the established order'. David Howe describes the development of social work during the second half of the nineteenth century as being created within 'the tension between the political and the personal' (1996, p. 81). This tension he argues results from the process and development of industrialization during the nineteenth century and the threat of rapid economic and social change posing a threat to social order. At this time, social work was one of a number of emerging occupations which were showing increasing interest in the experiences of individuals who were being alienated by, or left behind by the new emerging economic and social order:

> The 'social' was defined as that area in which personal relationships (family life, child-rearing practices, interpersonal behaviour) became of interest to the state, and the state's attitude to personal behaviour became relevant to the individual. The 'social' emerged as an area between the private and the public, a field in which the state penetrated the world of private relationships. (Howe 1996, p. 81)

Social work developed as a profession with a mandate to assess or judge the actions of others and to treat those actions – essentially a mandate to both care and control (Donzelot 1979; Oliver 1990; Parton 1994). Howe writes: 'Social work, therefore, formed and was thoroughly immersed in one of modernity's key projects – to bring discipline and order, progress and improvement to the human condition' (1996, p. 81).

The medical, biological, social and psychological sciences were also developing at this time, and provided the emerging profession of social work with 'scientific' explanations of 'problem' behaviours, as well as providing a means of classifying and categorizing different groups of people within the population. The main classificatory principles that were developing included:

- Age – the conceptualization of childhood and the principles of 'normal' development; adolescence; old age as characterised by dependency
- 'Able-bodiedness' – in the context of the development of categories of 'physical and mental impairment' which were seen as a disqualification from participation in social and economic activity
- Gender – the identification of the differentiating characteristics of men and women
- Sexuality – 'normal' and 'abnormal' sexualities, and the classification of homosexuality as a deviant condition
- Race – the identification of racial types, and the development of hierarchies of development. (adopted from Clarke 1993)

Each of these conditions developed its own specialist knowledge and expert practitioners, and each is own set of rules which helped to identify the difference between the 'normal' (independent and autonomous adults) and the 'abnormal' or 'deviant' minority requiring special attention (Clarke 1993, pp. 6–7)

This process of 'scientific' classification can be illustrated by looking at the 'social' and 'scientific' construction of the identity of people with learning difficulties. As has already been discussed, the nineteenth century saw rapid industrialization, and major demographic upheaval, underpinned by the development of capitalism.

Capitalism, it is argued

> ... put a premium on the classification and selection of the workforce in terms of speed and literacy and numeracy skills, and also upon the qualities deemed necessary for competent motherhood. Since people with learning difficulties failed on both counts, they have been largely excluded from the rewards and status of paid work and parenthood, and rendered marginal to society. (Williams 1989, p. 257)

The demands of wage labour in the capitalist economy had the consequence of identifying disability in general as individual pathology (Oliver 1990), whilst the emergence of compulsory education at the end of the nineteenth century played a significant part in identifying people with learning difficulties as 'a distinctive group and as a problem' (Ayer and Alaszewski 1984, p. 5). The concept of 'normality' developed in the nineteenth century by scientists and statisticians such as Galton (Hacking 1990) had the effect of describing as normal that which is most *typical*, and then asserts that this is the way that things *ought* to be.

The idea, or benchmark of the *average* thereby became a moral and social imperative: 'People with learning difficulties, from this point of view, are neither average nor normal' (Jenkins 1993, p. 18). Similarly claiming to have 'scientific' proof, the eugenics movement aimed to 'improve' the 'fitness' of the European population (or 'race') by discouraging the breeding of the 'unfit' and the 'inferior' (Jenkins 1993).

In Britain, the 1913 Mental Deficiency Act was in large part a response to this political, social and economic background; the Act led to the identification and 'grading' of the 'mentally deficient' and their institutionalization in hospitals or 'colonies' where they were segregated from the communities and families in the outside world. Under the terms of the Act, 'defective' women who gave birth to an illegitimate child, without any independent means of support could be sent to an institution. Many women, with and without learning difficulties have spent the majority of their lives in long-stay institutions under this clause. The aims of such a policy were very much in keeping with the predominant ideologies of class, 'race' and gender of the period (Alaszewski 1988; Ryan and Thomas 1980). The 1913 Mental Deficiency Act was not repealed until 1959. The policy of segregation and institutionalization came about not just because of a concern for these people's exclusion from waged labour, and their resulting dependency, but also to prevent them from having children and further damaging the race.

This historical perspective is useful as it not only illustrates the emergence of the 'social' in social work, but also demonstrates how contemporary social work practice still functions in the role of reflecting society's concerns about identified social 'problems' in society. Also, for example, in the context of the lives of people with learning difficulties, a historical perspective clearly demonstrates how what is considered 'good practice' today is in many ways a continuing attempt to make 'good' the damage and de-humanization done to and suffered by people with learning difficulties in the past, in the name of 'good professional practice'. Social workers were a part of these de-humanizing practices.

'Who' becomes a client is largely a socially determined matter, that is, the individual's behaviour, either because she has a 'social' problem, or is a problem to others, is of social interest: 'Never simply is it a matter between a social worker and the client ... what social workers do, and who they do it with are socially determined matters. Social work might therefore be seen as an activity carried out under social auspices' (Howe, 1979, p. 33).

Timms and Timms argue in a similar vein, 'the "social" in their title [referring to social workers] refers to the auspices under which they work, rather than to their field (working as it were with things social)' (1977, p. 17). Fowler makes the point more forcibly when he says, 'Social work ceases to be such when it fails to reflect the norms of the society it serves' (1975, p. 91). And similarly, Nokes writes: 'not withstanding the welfare practitioners' desire for professional autonomy, the welfare professions are rooted in the values of wider society ... there can be no complete withdrawal from the essential social nature of welfare practice' (1967, p. 111).

The following example illustrates the argument presented above. When someone has a toothache, the ache exists solely within the person, and its origins lie solely within the person (the decayed tooth). It is not (at least not directly) the result of, or dependent on, other people. It is matter of concern only for the sufferer and the dentist. Similarly, the dentist's knowledge-base and task of alleviating the toothache are not socially based, or carried out under 'social auspices'. However, in comparison, a social worker's response to a delinquent teenager is totally dependent on other people. First, it requires a 'socially determined' definition of who and what is or is not delinquent; second, the social worker's involvement with the delinquent is based on a social and moral response to the delinquency. That is, the creation of the 'social worker', the 'delinquent', and the social worker's response and responsibility to the delinquent all depend on and are derived from other people. Without this 'social interest', argues Howe, 'the individual's behaviour and conditions can be of no concern to the social worker qua social worker' (1979, p. 32).

However, none of the argument above in any way assumes (or is dependent on) that who or what is defined as a social problem is necessarily commonly agreed or recognized. In the first place, certain specific groups within society (for example, the government of the day) may be responsible for, and have the power and influence to define social problems. Second, who or what is defined as a social problem may change over time and in differing circumstances. What is important here is that 'human conduct and social reactions to it are political and moral in character' (Howe 1979, p. 33).

The importance of agency function

A second major consideration which comes out of this description of social work is the concept of agency function. Largely through the writings of the functionalist school of social work, the concept of agency function has attempted to describe the nature of the relationship between the individual (client), social worker and society. As the argument above has indicated, social workers are by definition neither autonomous nor private practitioners, just as clients are not 'abstracted individuals simply choosing between commodities' (Timms 1983, p. 81). Jessie Taft, one of the people who originally developed the concept of agency function, wrote of the agency as 'a background which holds both worker and client in a larger reality' (Taft 1944, in Timms 1983, p. 81). In this 'larger reality', the social worker is identified primarily with the tasks which society has sanctioned the agency to carry out, rather than with the client: 'The caseworker's responsibility on the other hand, real as it is, must first of all be to the agency and its functions; only as agency does he meet this client professionally' (Taft in Smalley 1967, p. 109). So, the 'social' in social work refers not just to its concern with social relationships – the relationship between the individual and society – but to the sanction and auspices for its practice. Social work has a social base and is not just a matter between social worker and client.

Winnicott describes the relationship between social work and agency function in terms of agency function having the role of a parent figure. For example, in child care she defines the agency's function as parental, expressing the sense of responsibility that exists in the community towards children. Similarly, she argues that the primary social function of probation workers is to offer their clients a corrective experience of authority which is 'reasonable, consistent and based on concern for the other person' (Winnicott 1964, p. 109).

Timms has also written about the central importance of agency function in social work:

> The agencies are established to carry out such broad social functions as healing and rehabilitation in the case of hospitals, ensuring good parental care in the case of children's departments of the local authority ... the most important aspect of agency function is that it constitutes the meeting point of social worker and client, it is what brings them together and gives meaning and sustenance to their continued contact. (Timms 1964, pp. 8–9)

Howe puts even greater emphasis on the importance of agency function by suggesting that social work has no identity outside agency function, denying it any degree of autonomy to determine its own identity, its task, who is the client, and the relationship with the client:

> To have social work embedded in society may be to preclude it having any discrete existence outside its relationship with various social agencies. The work of social work emerges out of social processes, the outcome of which determines who the clients are to be and how they are to be handled ... inbred with the 'social' at all levels, social work is unable to disentangle itself from the social world without ceasing to be social work. (Howe 1979, p. 35)

Social work's lack of power to 'determine' itself is echoed by Johnson (1977) who describes two basic areas of social work which are outside the control of social workers. First, there is the determination of clients and their needs (the problem), and second, the character of the responses available (the method). Both of these are identified and determined by the state.

Finally, Warham writes that 'real' social work (referring to local authority social service departments) can only be defined in relation to the social context in which social workers find themselves: 'It is not of a kind which is at the discretion of the profession itself to determine without reference to the essentially public nature of the situations in which social workers are employed' (1977, p. 52).

The argument here is that social work values operate within the 'agency' and its socially defined and sanctioned concerns. As such, analysis of values in social work must relate to the context in which they function, and must seek to locate their role and importance within this context. In order to do this it is necessary to examine in detail the nature of the social worker's role within this 'agency' 'socially sanctioned' context.

8 The social work role

Social work knowledge and values – creating the subject

As was seen in the previous chapter, social work draws on a number of different disciplines, particularly from within the social sciences, which attempt to create an 'objective' picture of the individual and society (for example, as in psychology and sociology). This 'objective' picture offers the possibility of categorization, classification and generalizations of human experience and behaviour, upon which 'appropriate' methods of interventions in individual's lives can be identified and implemented, by relevant agencies and professionals.

However, Mark Philp argues that whilst social work draws on this knowledge-base, the process and role of social work in society is to produce a knowledge of the individual as a 'subject': 'Social work produces a "subject in objective knowledge"' (1979, p. 91). Although, in creating the subject, social work draws on other disciplines, it differs from them and is not reducible to them because of its purpose and role of creating the 'subject'. Pearson suggests that 'social work emphatically embraces human subjectivity and regards itself as a carrier of the human tradition of compassion' (1975a, p. 128).

In terms of the relationship which the social worker has with the individual and with the state, social work can be seen as 'straddling a split' (Philp 1979, p. 92) between subjective states of the individual and their objective statuses. Subjective states may be characterized, for example, by pain, suffering, need, love and hate; objective statuses may be characterized by, for example, old age, disability, mental illness, learning difficulties, debts or crime, etc. The objective status of an individual is the result of social processes within society that identify areas of behaviour and experience as being of social interest, to which agency function responds.

The emergence of the identification of 'mental retardation' in the nineteenth century and the history of the development of the recognition of child abuse (Parton 1979) are examples of these processes. Against this (although still within the context of 'agency'), social work knowledge and its ensuing principles require the social worker to consider and represent (though not necessarily to act as advocate for) the subjective state of the socially identified and defined individual. The knowledge and value-base of the social worker transforms individual subjective states and objective statuses to create a 'social subject' (Philp 1979, p. 92). Importantly, from the point of view of a study of values in social work, the subject is characterized by her capacity to be a self-determining, responsible and sociable citizen (Plant 1970, Ch. 3).

Mediating between subjective and objective

Essentially, social work performs a mediating role in society, engaged through its knowledge of the subject of which its values are the focal point, in the recognition of social potential. As Pearson (1975a, p. 135) argues, 'social work theory and practice strive to give the deviant a voice', although this task, as we have seen, may be limited:

> It [social work] negotiates on behalf of the mad, bad, and the stigmatised; between those who have been excluded from power and those who have the power to exclude between the sound in body and the handicapped, between the law abiding and the law breaking and the sane and the borderline. (Philp 1979, p. 97)

Philp describes social work as developing historically between two discourses, the discourse of wealth and the discourse of poverty. The first 'form' of social work was composed of a discourse of charity in which the charity worker mediated between the privileged and the poor, representing the humanity of the privileged to the poor, and the essential 'goodness' of the poor to the privileged. At present, social work 'occupies the space between the respectable and the deviant' (Philp 1979, p. 96). In the same vein, David Howe describes social work as operating on the edges of different worlds – the world of the individual and the world of those with the power to legislate how behaviour is to be judged: 'The social worker mediates and translates between these various worlds' (Howe 1979, p. 43; see also Howe 1996).

Martin Davies describes the role of the social worker as one of reconciliation in which the social worker is concerned with maintaining the individual and society, and with negotiating the interdependent relationship between the individual and society:

> The social worker is contributing towards the maintenance of society by exercising some control over deviant members and allocating scarce resources according to policies laid down by the state but implemented on an individual basis. She is maintaining members in society by exercising control by allocating resources designed to maximize self-respect and develop the abilities of individuals to survive under their own steam. (Davies 1994, p. 58)

According to Davies, the 'maintenance strategy' has two main aspects. On the one hand, social workers are employed by the state to control and monitor excesses of behaviour which society classes as deviant. For example, social workers are involved in preventing child abuse, the compulsory admission to hospital of mentally ill individuals, and recommending the reception of 'problem' children into care. Another aspect to mediation is a concern with 'ameliorating the living conditions' of those who are finding it difficult to cope without help. So, for example, the social worker might work to improve the quality of life for unemployed teenagers, disabled people and individuals with emotional and relationship difficulties: 'All of these acts are intended to contribute to a smooth-running society, to maintain it' (Davies 1994, p. 58).

The creation of subjects is essential to both of these aspects of mediation, and also to a further aspect of mediation described by Philp (1979). In presenting the potential of the subject, the social worker is suggesting that the objective status, which has cast the individual as a client in the first place, can be integrated into the subject. This integration is necessary, he argues, for the return to the individual of their full discursive rights. The objective status removes from the client the rights to normal discourse and can only be returned by a process (of negotiation or mediation) whereby subjective status is gradually returned. This role of the social worker and the process of mediation can be well illustrated in symbolic form below (adapted from Philp 1979).

If a child A commits an offence B and is brought before the court, he will be seen (legally) through his objective status as B(a). That is, he will be seen principally as an offender and only second as an individual. If the offence is not serious, the social worker may be able to present a picture of the subject (in the court report) that transforms B(a) into A(b), so that the offence is seen as secondary to the individual's subjective characteristics. If the offence is more serious, or previous offences have been committed, the child may be made the subject of supervision, in which the child's B status will fade, and he will again be accepted as A if after a time he does not commit offence B again during this period. The social worker may use various forms of 'treatment' which help the social worker to present a 'scientific or objective picture of the process of change in a client to other discourses – essentially those "explanations" serve to change the client's status from B(a) to A(b)' (Philp 1979, p. 101).

The length of the whole process of integration and the extent to which it can be completed, given the limitations to the acceptance of the 'subjective', depends on the nature and extent of the objective status. This can be illustrated by the following examples.

If someone asks a social worker to liaise with one of the fuel boards over the non-payment of a bill (and perhaps a threat of disconnection), probably to try to negotiate some arrangement of weekly repayments, then the whole process would most likely be fairly short and straightforward. If, however, a parent is suspected of neglecting their child (as in the case of Sheila and David), then the anxiety, fear and censure present in such a referral is such that the social worker's involvement is liable to be quite a lengthy process.

In the process of integration the social worker, as well as trying to negotiate the client's objective characteristics into a subject, may also be trying to integrate them into wider society. The social worker attempts to change perceptions both in the client and in those around the client: 'The more powerful those characteristics are, the more likely it is, that the process will take place with the individual, the less strong, the more easily will the integration be effective in those around the client' (Philp 1979, p. 101).

Social work values and creating the subject

Social work values are central to the creation of the subject, providing the 'subjective' focus within which the social worker operates. Here the most basic value or 'prerequisite to having values at all' (Plant 1970, p. 12) is respect for persons (individualization), the 'recognition of the value and dignity of every human being irrespective of origin, race, status, sex, sexual orientation, age, disability, belief, or contribution to society' (BASW 1996, para. 6). This value base requires the social worker to appreciate how the individual perceives and experiences her world. The 'subject' and the social worker's relationship with the subject are based on 'the inherent worth of man [sic] … independent of his actual achievements or behaviour' (Butrym 1976, p. 43).

The social worker, on the one hand faced with, for example, an 'objectified' vandal, and on the other with a legal discourse, attempts to present the underlying subjectivity of the vandal. The social worker describes the underlying character, the essential good, 'the authentic and the unalienated ... in doing so he is producing a picture of the vandal as a subject who is not immediately visible, but who exists as a potential, a possibility, a future social being' (Philp 1979, p. 99).

Interestingly, Biestek argues along similar lines, though much earlier and from a theological standpoint in the last few pages of his book, particularly where he describes the value of 'individualization': 'the recognition of and understanding of each client's right and need to be treated as an individual who has unique qualities' (1974, p. 136).

In the conclusions to their research into practice theories of social work, Curnock and Hardiker (1979) describe the nature of the social work task in relation to assessing referrals, and writing social inquiry reports:

> However typical or general a client's situation and problems seem to be, a way has to be found of finding out what they mean to that particular person. Individualisation is the theoretical key which helps us to be rather more specific about the 'making sense process'. (Curnock and Hardiker 1979, p. 165)

Here, they are referring to the importance of creating the 'subject', of understanding the subjective experience of the individual, central to which is the value of individualization (deriving from respect for persons). They go on to describe how, in order to make an assessment or come to any conclusions about the individual, it is necessary to individualize the presenting problems (crime, abuse, mental illness, etc.) in relation to the client's life situation, such as 'strengths and stresses in his personal or social circumstances' (1979, p. 165).

Whilst acknowledging the radical critique of individualization ('respect for persons', as discussed in Part I), Curnock and Hardiker describe the concept as helping social workers to make sense of some of the processes that they are involved in as they make assessments as part of their social inquiries.

Limitations

Both Philp and Howe have pointed out that the individual can only be regarded as a subject if they 'do not have any overpowering objective or narcissistic characteristics' (Philp 1979, p. 92); and 'if that [socially identified] behaviour becomes too far removed from the way things ought to be, it is dealt with as alien, threatening and in need of sharp control' (Howe 1979, pp. 42–3).

Thus the social worker's relationship with the individual (client) is limited, that is, society's commitment to allowing a subjective picture of the individual to emerge from within their objective status is tolerated only within socially sanctioned boundaries. The social worker cannot speak for those whose objective status overwhelms their subjectivity. The objective description and status of a child abuser or 'experienced' delinquent may well outweigh the social worker's 'subjective' interest in the person, their 'inherent worth', their 'value and dignity', irrespective of their achievements or behaviour, and their right to be self-determining. The subjective description will not be heard when

> ... the objective characteristics of the feared outweigh all the subjective possibilities ... social work is allocated those whose objective status is not too threatening ... it cannot operate, it cannot make people when an individual's act has removed him from the right to be perceived as human. (Philp 1979, p. 98)

For example, the social worker cannot defend the mass murderer or the 'florid psychotic', because their objective status is so great as to overwhelm their subjectivity. In the case of an adolescent in court for his fourth 'burglary' offence, and who has already been in care, his objective status will probably be considered greater than his subjective characteristics or potential by the magistrates, and he may receive a custodial sentence.

However, the socially sanctioned boundaries within which social work takes place are not static, and there is a constant tension between social work, dealing with people who are objectively defined as being of interest and concern to society, and dealing with those same people in 'the subjective' as individuals worthy of individual 'respect' and 'concern'. This tension becomes apparent in what seem to be society's contradictory expectations of social work, such as care and control, although as Fowler (1975) and Davies (1994) point out, both are integral and important social work functions in the context of agency function.

There is also another limitation that it is important to address here, that draws on the radical critique of social work and its value base (see Chapter 3), and that adds an important qualification to both Philp's and Davies' analyses. Whilst it may be the role of social work in society to identify and work with the 'subject', within a 'maintenance' role, the success of social work carrying out this role can be questioned. Certainly from the perspective of the radical critique, it can be argued that social work is itself a part of the process of 'objectifying' (pathologizing) individuals – of being a part of the process of confirming an individual's 'objective status' – in instances where the social work response does not accommodate and respond to the wider contextual ('subjective') understandings of the client.

Does the social worker's response to the suspected case of parental neglect of a child respond to the 'dangerousness' of the child's situation, focusing on the 'abusing' parent and the requirement for close 'monitoring' and 'control'? In essence, is the social worker's response a part of the process of identifying and confirming the parent's 'objective' status? Or does the social worker's response address wider, or underlying questions and issues that may be factors in explaining the abuse or level of 'risk' in the situation, in essence seeking, identifying and working with the parent as the 'subject'? Steve Rogowski (1991) gives a case example of a child with a black eye referred to a social worker, with the obvious implications and questions about physical abuse of the child, and 'risk'. The social worker's response during her assessment and work with the parent, however, was to focus on the difficult social and economic context of the parent's (mother's) situation, which was the major source of the stress within the family and had resulted in the physical abuse. This is not to suggest that the social worker's role is simply one of choosing to 'objectify' the client or choosing to work with the client as a 'subject', acknowledging the wider contextual understandings of their life and actions. The case of Sheila and David, presented in Part II, illustrates that social work is more complex than this, and involves the social worker 'juggling' with many levels and perspectives in working with their clients. However, the argument here does suggest that social work may also be a part of the process of identifying the 'objective status' of the individual as well as identifying and working with the 'subjective characteristics' of the individual.

There are also critical questions to be addressed deriving from this argument and the social work role of 'maintenance'. Whilst it may describe the nature of the role of social work in society, it may also be a part of the 'objectification' and 'pathologization' of individuals, depending on the agency remit that the social worker is working within. For example, 'the social worker 'maintains' or supports people with learning difficulties to live as independently as possible in the community, for example by providing 'ordinary housing'. But if the social, economic barriers, and discrimination in society that work against the genuine acceptance and 'inclusion' of people with learning difficulties in society, their communities and neighbourhoods are not also addressed, then that is a failure to address the major ways in which society (informally as well as in policy and professional attitudes) continue to 'objectify' and marginalize people with learning difficulties.

Summary

The role of the social worker is to speak for the 'subject' within the 'object'. She is sanctioned by society, through her employing agency, to speak for the subject, and for someone who can return again to their subjective status although, for example, in the case of older people and disabled people (as suggested in the example of people with learning difficulties above), this may not reduce or nullify their objective characteristics. The extent to which this task is possible, though, is limited by society, its norms and its expectations of the social services agency; it is also a part of the social worker's role to represent those norms and expectations. So although it is the social worker's role to represent the 'subjective' characteristics of the individual, it is not necessarily her role to act as an advocate 'for and on behalf' of the client. It is the social worker's role to represent and translate the subjective experience of the individual to society, and society's norms and expectations to the individual, and maintain a 'society'-determined balance between the two. Hence the social worker's role is complex, as it essentially includes aspects of both care and control.

Who becomes a client in the first place is largely determined by society, and depending on the extent of the individual's objective status, the social worker may be acting for society more than the individual.

Social work values (principally 'respect for persons') are of central importance to this description of social work, because they are of central importance to the creation of the subject. Without values ('respect for persons'), there can be no subject, and without the subject, there can be no social work. However, this is not to say that social work's values are necessarily always the dominant values in evidence. Society's values may, in fact, overrule them, and do at least determine the extent to which their 'voice' can be heard in the creation of the subject. Society also determines the extent to which the social worker is able, or is sanctioned, to promote the expressed wishes of the client.

For example, although social work places a high value on promoting (in theory) the client's right to self-determination (as negative freedom), as has been argued and illustrated above, no such right is tenable in an absolute form. It is limited by the interests of 'parties' other than the client, in which the social worker's role may be one of social control through regulating the acceptable or permissible extent of client self-determination. This was illustrated by both of the case studies in Part II. The client's right to self-determination is also limited by the social worker's concern for the interests of the client, even where this may contradict the client's own wishes (self-determination as positive freedom justifying the denial of self-determination as negative freedom, as in the case of Mrs M).

Although the commitment to self-determination is an important one in social work value theory, in practice, social workers work within a social context in which some of their tasks are designed to monitor and procure social control. Clarke with Asquith comment that: 'Social workers perhaps sense that in a way they are expected to be on both sides of the self-determination – social control, and self-determination – paternalism boundaries at the same time' (1985, p. 40). As has been argued, social work is not an autonomous or independent profession. It exists under social auspices and as such its clients and its role with them is sanctioned and determined by society through agency function. This is the context in which social work values exist and operate.

9 Values, social work and contexts

The main argument has been that in order to examine and understand social work values, it is necessary to understand the nature of social work and the social worker's relationship with society. It is not sufficient simply to look at values in the context of the relationship between the social worker and the client. That is, it is not sufficient to consider only the theoretical or 'professional' description of social work values as if they existed in a 'case-work vacuum'. Parts II and III, through practice illustrations and analysis, showed that 'outside factors' – the context in which the interaction between social worker and client takes place – plays an important role in determining and understanding the place and practical operation of social work values. In Part III, the main function of social work has been described as creating 'subjects', central to which lies the basic social work value of 'respect for persons' (individualization).

However, in this description, the way in which values are used and work is essentially 'instrumental'. That is, they are instrumental to achieving the end of creating the subject. It is this task of the social worker and social work values which describes and determines (within agency-defined limits) the nature of the social worker's relationship with the client.

The 'end' of creating the subject is itself sanctioned and determined by agency function which reflects the norms and expectations of society. Within this, respect for persons provides the 'means' by which the social worker creates and presents a picture of the 'subjective' characteristics of the client as an individual. However, it might also be the case that social work is at times, with intent or by default, a part of the process of identifying and confirming the 'objective' status of individuals.

Within this description of social work, values are basically instrumental to the purpose, and appear to be no more than a 'means to an end', of creating 'subjects'. They are not 'absolute' imperatives, as was illustrated in the case of Mrs M's limited rights to self-determination.

To complete this analysis of values in social work, it is worth considering three related issues or questions. The first raises the issues of whether social work's value-base should be something more than just 'instrumental'. The second issue considers the place of social work's value-base in the light of descriptions of social work as an increasingly fragmented profession. Third, and related to the first two issues is the question of how the value-base of social work might be taken forward as social work develops; and in a way that addresses some of the problems associated with the concept of 'respect for persons'. It is not intended to attempt to provide 'clear-cut answers' here. It is probably evident from the analysis above that such an attempt would at the very best be superficial. Rather, it is intended that this final chapter in this exploration of social work values prompts the reader to explore and question further the role and application of social work values, particularly (where relevant) as it relates to the readers' own social work practice.

'Values are not instrumental to some purpose, but are expressive of some ultimate conviction'?

As mentioned above, it appears from this description of social work that values are basically instrumental to the purpose, and appear to be no more than a 'means to an end', of creating 'subjects'. However, this particular description raises the important question: 'Is this all that there is to say about social work values?' Or are values, as Ruth Wilkes claims, 'not instrumental to some purpose, but expressive of some ultimate conviction' (1981, p. 64)? The answer, not surprisingly perhaps, is more complex than can be formulated by an 'either/or' question. The question, though, is important because behind this claim of Wilkes lie many generally held basic assumptions about social work as a 'profession' with a clear set of values.

Deontological and utilitarian values

The conclusions to Part I briefly described how local authority-based social work is founded on a utilitarian concept of need. Clarke with Asquith (1985, p. 70) argue that certainly since the Seebohm Report (1968) social work has been based on such a conception. The report called for a reorganization of the personal social services to attract more resources, and to meet needs on the basis of the overall requirements of the family, or individual. Having a 'need' implies lacking a 'good' whose possession is, in an important way, conducive to 'happiness'. From this it is the task of social work to attempt to maximize the well-being of individuals and that of the community as a whole. Similarly Martin Davies (1994, pp. 57–72), in describing the role of social work as 'maintenance' – ['Social workers'] ... acts are intended to contribute to a smooth running society' – also appears to be describing a strong utilitarian commitment to the development of social work. Again, Ruth Wilkes has written 'consciously or unconsciously, social work thinking is for the most part, sympathetic with utilitarian modes of thought in that the worth of a policy or action is measured against its tendency to produce "good" results' (Wilkes 1981, p. 63).

A description of social work principally depicting the role of 'respect for persons' as being instrumental in the creation of subjects would appear to fit neatly into a description of social work with a strong utilitarian base, in which the 'end' rather than any moral obligation is the justification for the act. And it certainly accords with a description of social work as an activity which is practised under the auspices and sanctions of society.

However, this view of social work and is values contrasts sharply with the more 'traditional' description and the role of social work values, particularly respect for persons, as described in Part I. An assertion of the value of each individual person clearly contrasts with the 'utilitarian' promotion of the 'common good'. Commenting on this, Clarke with Asquith say that: 'if respect for persons is more than an empty professional formula, it seems to commit social work to a deontological morality' (1985, p. 77). In the context of the description of social work and social work values given in Part III, it is difficult to accommodate this statement from Clarke with Asquith, but like the earlier quotation from Wilkes ('values are not instrumental ... but expressive of some ultimate conviction'), it seems to suggest that there is some 'absolute value truth' which is (or should be) fundamental and necessary to social work practice. Unfortunately, examination of this issue is often clouded and confused because, as for example in the quotation from Clarke with Asquith, such value talk is related to the often vague and mostly superficially used notion of 'professional' in social work: 'professional guidelines', 'professional values', 'professional responsibilities', etc. To properly analyse what 'professional' means in the context of social work goes beyond the scope of the discussion here, apart from a brief look at it in relation to the description of social work that has been developed.

Butrym (1976) lists four elements that are basic to professionalism in social work:

1 Service orientation – not putting the worker's interests before those of the client
2 The social usefulness of social work
3 Enhanced effectiveness
4 Responsibilities held by professionals in trust for society.

This conception of social work is based on three assumptions:

1 There is a distance between the state and the professional
2 The profession has significant independence, and is apart from direct political control
3 Social work operates within only a broad social mandate.

According to Part III, this conception of social work as a profession is based on a myth, albeit a powerful one, which, in order to establish social work with 'professional' status and credibility, ignores or at least seriously underestimates and misunderstands the relationship between social work and society. Social work is 'social' work and is practised directly and closely under social auspices, through a precise social mandate, and is subject to direct political control. Unlike other 'care' professions such as medicine and dentistry, social work is inextricably linked with the society which sanctions it, and which it serves.

What is significant is that within much of the use of the concept of 'professional', social work values are conceptualized as being 'absolute', that is, they are conceptualized in a deontological way (for example, as can be seen in the quotations above from Wilkes and Clarke with Asquith). This is to the extent that in as much as social work is a utilitarian enterprise, it is seen (if acknowledged at all) as being somehow separate from the 'absolute' value-base of 'professional' social work practice. The argument here is that no such separation is possible. It is not possible to separate the 'form' of social work values from the way in which they work in practice.

Deontological and utilitarian values in context

While a deontologist might argue it is inherently right to maintain an elderly person in the community as long as possible (in terms of respecting her 'rights' and choice to do so), a utilitarian might justify placing the person in residential care on the grounds that, in the long run, this will result in less of a burden for the person's family (a desirable consequence) (Reamer 1982, p. 17).

Although this example falls into the 'either/or' trap, it does illustrate the moral complexity of social work. Although social work may be described as a largely utilitarian enterprise, its values and how they work are not so readily described as being either utilitarian or deontological, as the example suggests. The 'reality' is that, although a social worker would normally try to maintain an elderly person in the community for as long as possible (as in the case illustration of Mrs M in Part II), there may also come a time (as in the case of Mrs M) when the consequences of this on herself and others outweighs the elderly person's ability and right to remain in the community. It should be remembered that the social worker's role is to represent the interests and concerns of society as well as those of the individual, and within a discretionary space, mediate between the two. From this one cannot say, as according to the quotations from Clarke with Asquith, Wilkes and Reamer above, that the values of 'respect for persons' and 'client self-determination' are 'absolute values', or are to be regarded or used deontologically. In the context in which local authority social work is practised this is not possible. The social worker is essentially mediating between the individual and society, and in this context the power or authority of social work values is essentially discretionary, and their 'absolute' work or applicability is subject to the interest and tolerance of society.

However, it would be equally false to claim (as in the quotation from Clarke with Asquith) that because of this, respect for persons is no more than an 'empty professional formula'. It is not empty because it is essential to the social work task of creating subjects, and without it there can be no social work. Without respect for persons (individualization), there can be no subject. Without the 'subject', there is no social work. But, because social work is carried out under social auspices, in terms of determining the lives of individuals, social work values such as client self-determination are necessarily limited. Whilst one might in one sense describe as 'absolute' the social work task of creating subjects, the objective status of some individuals might in fact be greater than their subjective characteristics, and it is a part of the social work task to act according to society's mandate (which determines agency function) where this is the case, as it was in the case illustration of Mrs M.

Therefore, whilst respect for persons is essential to the creation of subjects, because of social workers' dependence on a 'social mandate', and the nature of the social work task itself, respect for persons does not provide the individual as client any rights within the client/social worker relationship.

Statements such as:

Social work is a professional activity. Implicit in its practice are ethical principles which prescribe the professional responsibility of the social worker. The primary objective of the code is to make these implicit principles explicit for the protection of clients and other members of society. (BASW 1996) are at best confusing, and at worst simply do not make sense. In the context of local authority social work, this quotation from BASW, and the earlier quotation from Reamer both fall short of understanding and relating in a clear sense to the complexity of the social work role in society.

References to 'clients" rights, and to 'professional' are problematical at the least because they are based on the idea of 'professional' being synonymous with 'independent' and 'autonomous'. This may be the case regarding some professions, but it certainly is not the case regarding social work. So to speak of values existing in the same vein is misguided.

To return to the quotation from Wilkes ('values are not instrumental ... but expressive of some ultimate conviction'); one could argue that whilst values are instrumental to the task of creating subjects, and as such they may be held to be expressive of a central social work conviction; this conviction is also limited as it exists only within the boundaries of the extent to which society sanctions it. In other words this conviction is not ultimate in any 'absolute' sense, any more than the nature of a particular society is absolute. It is society's conviction to and interest in the subjective characteristics of certain people living on its margins that determines precisely what it means and how far it can be taken within social work practice.

It is clear from this that 'values in social work' is a considerably more complex and difficult area of study than has often been acknowledged. Traditionally 'values' have been studied and written about primarily in the context of the relationship between the social worker and client, mostly ignoring the relationship between the social worker and society. However, in order to understand values, how they are used, and how they work in practice (within the social worker/client relationship), one has to acknowledge and examine the context in which this relationship takes place. That is, one has to examine and take account of the social worker's relationship with society, which itself sanctions, determines, defines, limits and gives meaning to the social worker/client relationship.

Social work – a fragmenting profession?

As a profession, social work is constantly evolving, which is itself a reflection of the close relationship between the profession and the society in which it exists, and which gives it its mandate for practice. In recent years however, a number of commentators and analysts of social work have argued that as a profession, social work has become increasingly fragmented, for example, Howe 1994, 1996; Parton 1994; Dominelli 1996. This 'fragmentation' is explained as resulting from a number of political and policy-based shifts in direction during the 1980s, and increasing doubts being expressed during the 1970s and 1980s about the effectiveness of welfare provision. Social work has often been one of the main targets of much of the criticisms levelled at the welfare state:

> The changes in social work are part of a much broader set of changes which some have characterised as symptomatic of 'postmodernism' ... relating to the crisis of confidence in the welfare state, cutbacks in public sector resources, privatisation and marketisation of public services, decentralisation of services and budgets, the growth of a new managerialism focusing on economy, effectiveness and efficiency and a general deprofessionalising trend. (Banks 1996, p. 118).

John Clarke (1996) in his analysis of developments in social work identifies the development of marketization, mixed economies of welfare, a transfer of 'care' responsibilities from 'formal' to 'informal' provision, and the growth of 'managerialism' as key aspects of change. One result of this has been an increase in specialisms in social work, in a move away from the notion of the 'generic' social worker. Banks (1996) also identifies the growth in the development of government, and agency guidelines and procedures, for example, in the areas of assessment in child protection and community care provision, and the rise of 'consumerism', as offering challenges to what she sees as the 'traditional' roles of the social worker.

Whilst these changes, and shifts in emphasis in contemporary social work practice are undeniable, there is a danger (as recognized by Clarke 1996) that the 'break' that it is sometimes suggested that they have with social work 'as it was' is overemphasized and/or based on a false idea of what social work actually was:

> ... there is a danger here of projecting a past in which social work was authoritative and received deferentially or acquiescently by those subjected to it. But this will not do. Social work's past is marked by challenges, resistances and refusals in both collective and individual forms. From its nineteenth-century origins, social work has been viewed ambiguously and sceptically by both its beneficiaries and commentators on it. (Clarke 1996, p. 43)

The key question that arises here, with respect to social work values, is the 'universal' ethical base of social work, for example, is the BASW's *Code of Ethics* (1996) still relevant in the light of these developments in social work, particularly with respect to its suggested 'fragmentation'? There are two aspects to answering this question.

First, the potential answer to this question partly lies in what one's initial opinion of social work was or is. If one accepts Clarke's scepticism, and much of the argument and analysis of this book, then one is initially led to question the extent to which the current developments and changes in social work signify a radical shift in the nature of social work practice. Social work always has been and probably always will be a complex profession, constantly open to negotiation and renegotiation as society's priorities and values change themselves. In the context of social work in the United Kingdom, most of which is carried out under the auspices of local authority social service departments, the profession of social work has never been autonomous, 'has [always] been viewed ambiguously', and has never simply been a matter of negotiation between the client and the social worker. So, whilst aspects of the organization and language of social work may change, as indeed they have, the argument here is that the essential mediation role of social work is still relevant today in understanding the nature and role of social work in society.

If one accepts that this is the case then the nature of our questions regarding the adequacy and relevance of social work's ethical base today need to focus on this 'defining' mediation role of social work in society. The starting point for the questioning is a recognition of a continuum of change and development in the organization of social work rather than what some perceive today as being a radical break from the past.

Second, from the perspective of the trend for social work to reorganize into areas of specialist practice, for example, child protection, mental health, community care services, etc., one needs to ask whether the role and function of the social worker in any one of these separate areas is sufficiently 'unique' from other areas of practice to suggest that there is a requirement for a 'different morality' (Banks 1996, p. 127) as a base for that practice? There are dangers here, alluded to in Chapter 1 in the discussion of how the concept of 'respect for persons' might be 'adapted' or in effect diluted in its moral import so that it may apply to persons not recognized as having rationality or being able to act autonomously, etc. A main danger is that certain identities and certain vulnerable people in certain situations may be subject to practice based on a professional value-base that itself does not fully respect their human and societal rights.

Similarly, it is possible that a value-base may be developed that first and foremost focuses on the needs of the professional service providers, and service context, rather than those of the service users. This is not to deny earlier arguments made that were critical of the application of 'respect for persons' as the basic ethic of social work (which I will return to shortly), but it is to recognize the (potential) value of a universal ethic that is able to form the basis of respect for all clients/service users, and is strong enough to protect the client, whatever their identity, and in whatever area of the social work service that they might come into contact. Referring to the continuing survival of a universal code of ethics for social work, Sarah Banks writes:

> It may be important to hold on to this [code of ethics] not so much because of the fragmentation of the occupational group, but because proceduralisation, agency rules and codes of practice [are] increasing the danger of the social worker becoming nothing more than a technician or official. New consumerist or radical approaches may have something to offer in the future, but at the present time they do not do enough to prevent the insidious rise of defensive practice. (Banks 1996, p. 128)

'Respect for persons' – in context?

Inasmuch as the argument in the last section cautions against abandoning a universal code of ethics/value-base for social work, it begs the questions raised in Part I, particularly Chapter 3, regarding the adequacy of 'respect for persons' as the basic ethic for social work.

Is it the case that 'respect for persons' is not appropriate to social work, and an alternative formulation needs to be found, or is it more easily (perhaps) a matter of interpreting and using it in a way that addresses the criticisms made of it? Briefly, the main criticism identifies 'respect for persons' with its primary focus on the relationship between the client and the social worker, as not sufficiently acknowledging and accounting for the social context in which this relationship takes place. This has three related consequences:

- It hides the social context of their lives, for example, low income, unemployment, poor housing, etc.
- It ignores possible structural inequalities and processes that create the individual's social context, and therefore play a part in causing the problems (such as low income, etc.) that the individual faces.
- It can lead to the 'blaming' of the individual for the problems that they face, by focusing on their inability to cope with their situation, rather than seeing their problems as a result of structural inequalities in society.

A consequence of this decontextualization of the individual/client is that their identity and needs are at risk of being pathologized (and may be realized), in that the 'problem' is seen as lying within, or 'is' the individual/client themselves. It is evident from these criticisms that for 'respect for persons' to form the basis of the social worker's relationship with the client, whilst avoiding the negative consequences listed above, an understanding of the social (structural, political, cultural, etc.) contexts of the client (including the process and identity of being a 'client') must be a part of and inform that relationship. The social worker also needs to be aware of their own 'social construction' and professional role in the context of the agency and societal expectations of them as a social worker. It may also be the case that, where the societal expectations have a foundation in prejudice or ignorance, for the social worker to 'respect the client' she will have to challenge those expectations.

This all presents a difficult (but necessary) task for the social worker, not least because of the demand that she be able to interpret and practice 'respect' in ways that acknowledge the many different contexts and experiences of her clients. In essence, this is a model that maintains the validity of a universal imperative to 'respect persons' (which can be defined in terms of fundamental human rights), but also demands that the 'realization' of respect must accommodate 'locally contingent' factors, presented by the client's identity, experiences and needs; and the context of the social worker's relationship with the client.

In this model the use of 'respect for persons' is continually held up to scrutiny, as its use is explicit, rather than implicit or assumed, and continuously problematical. That it is continuously problematical is necessary, given the complexities of social work, and so it is important that it is recognized as such. Without this recognition there is the constant danger that:

> Doing one's duty may be mere compliance: an habitual and ultimately habituated application of generalised responses to a particular instance. Morally engaged practitioners could not hide within this professional ethical anesthesia, but would retain their responsibility for their professional practice and its implications. (Husband 1995, p. 87)

Finally, the message in this quote from Charles Husband is crucial. Social work as a profession is complex, as are the 'ethical' demands made of social workers. It is because of this that social workers constantly need to examine their practice, their roles, their relationships and the many different expectations of them. The value-base and professional code of ethics for social work do not provide any (easy) solutions in practice, or even at times clear guidelines that can be referred to in identifying the 'best' course of action. Depending on one's perspective, social work's values never will be able to, given the complex nature of social work. Perhaps because of this complexity, they never should, as this might reflect the rigid expectations of a highly restrictive model of practice. It is therefore important that there is an acceptance of this 'uncertainty', and that social workers become, as Charles Husband (1995) argues, 'morally engaged' and 'morally active practitioners'.

Bibliography

Alaszewski, A. (1988), 'From villians to victims', in Leighton, A. (ed.), *Mental Handicap in the Community*, London: Woodford Faulkner.

Ayer, S. and Alaszewski, A. (1984), *Community care and the mentally handicapped: services for mothers and their mentally handicapped children*, London: Croom Helm.

Ahmad, B. (1990), *Black Perspectives in Social Work*, Birmingham: Venture Press.

Anderson, D. (1982), *Social Work and Mental Handicap*, London: Macmillan.

Azmi, S. (1997), 'Professionalism and Social Diversity', in Hugman, R., Peelo, M. and Soothill, K. (eds), *Concepts of Care: Developments in Health and Social Welfare*, London: Edward Arnold.

Bailey, R. and Brake, M. (eds) (1975), *Radical Social Work*, London: Edward Arnold.

Banks, S. (1995), *Ethics and Values in Social Work*, Basingstoke: Macmillan.

Banks, S. (1996), 'Communities, Consumers and Codes: Ethical Issues in Social Work', in Parker, P. (ed.), *Ethics and Community*, University of Central Lancashire: Centre for Professional Ethics.

British Association of Social Workers (1996), *A Code of Ethics for Social Work*, Birmingham: BASW.

British Association of Social Workers (1977), *The Social Work Task*, Birmingham: BASW.

Berlin, I. (1969), 'Two Concepts of Liberty', in *Four Essays on Liberty*, Milton Keynes: Open University Press.

Bernstein, S. (1975), 'Self Determination: King or Citizen in the Realm of Values', in McDermott, F.E. (ed.), *Self-Determination in Social Work*, London: Routledge & Kegan Paul.

Biestek, F.P. (1974), *The Casework Relationship*, London: Allen and Unwin.

Braye, S. and Preston-Shoot, M. (1995), *Empowering Practice in Social Care*, Buckingham: Open University Press.

Budgen, R.P. (1982), 'A Critical Examination of the Principle of Self Determination in Social Work', University of East Anglia: unpublished Ph.D. thesis.

Butrym, Z. (1976), *The Nature of Social Work*, London: Macmillan.

Central Council for Education and Training in Social Work. (1976), Paper 13: *Values in Social Work*, London: CCETSW.

Central Council for Education and Training in Social Work. (1985), Paper 20.3: *Policies for Qualifying Training in Social Work: The Council's Propositions*, London: CCETSW.

Central Council for Education and Training in Social Work (1989), *Requirements and Regulations for the Diploma in Social Work*, London: CCETSW.

Central Council for Education and Training in Social Work. (1991), Paper 30: *Rules and Regulations for the Diploma in Social Work* (2nd edn), London: CCETSW.

Central Council for Education and Training in Social Work (1995), *Assuring Quality. Rules and Regulations for the Diploma in Social Work* (revised 1995), London: CCETSW.

Channon, G. (1974), 'Values and Professional Social Work', *Australian Social Work*, 27 (1), pp. 5–14.

Clarke, J. (ed.) (1993), *A Crisis in Care? Challenges to Social Work*, Milton Keynes: The Open University.

Clarke, J. (1996), 'After social work', in Parton, N. (ed.), *Social Theory, Social Change and Social Work*, London: Routledge.

Clarke, C. with Asquith, S. (1985), *Social Work and Social Philosophy, A Guide for Practice*, London: Routledge & Kegan Paul.

Corrigan, P. and Leonard, P. (1978), *Social Work Practice under Capitalism: A Marxist Approach*, London: Macmillan.

Curnock, K. and Hardiker, P. (1979), *Towards Practice Theory: Skills and Methods in Social Assessments*, London: Routledge & Kegan Paul.

Davies, M. (1994), *The Essential Social Worker: A Guide to Positive Practice*, Aldershot: Ashgate Publishing Company.

Dingwall, R. (1986), 'The Jasmine Beckford Affair', *The Modern Law Review*, 49, pp. 489–507.

Dingwall, R., Eekelaar, J.M. and Murray, T. (1983), *The Protection of Children*, Oxford: Blackwell.

Dominelli, L. (1988), *Anti-Racist Social Work*, Basingstoke: Macmillan.

Dominelli, L. (1996), 'Deprofessionalizing Social Work: Anti-oppressive Practice, Competencies and Postmodernism', *British Journal of Social Work*, 26, pp. 153–75.

Dominelli, L. and McLeod, E. (1989), *Feminist Social Work*, Basingstoke: Macmillan.

Donzelot, J. (1979), *The Policing of Families*, London: Hutchinson.

Downie, R.S. and Telfer, E. (1969), *Respect for Persons*, Sydney: Allen and Unwin.

Downie, R.S. and Telfer, E. (1980), *Caring and Curing: A Philosophy of Medicine and Social Work*, London: Methuen.

Downie, R.S. and Loudfoot, E.M. (1978), 'Aim, Skill and Role in Social Work', in Timms, N. and Watson, D. (eds), *Philosophy in Social Work*, London: Routledge & Kegan Paul.

Fairbairn, G. (1985), 'Responsibility in Social Work', in Watson, D. (ed.), *A Code of Ethics for Social Work, the 2nd Step*, London: Routledge & Kegan Paul.

Fowler, D.A. (1975), 'Ends and Means', in Jones, H. (ed.), *Towards a New Social Work*, London: Routledge & Kegan Paul.

Hacking, I. (1990), *The taming of chance*, Cambridge: Cambridge University Press.

Hollis, F. (1940), *Social Casework in Practice*, New York: Family Service Association of America.

Hollis, F. (1967), 'Principles and Assumptions Underlying Casework Practice', in Younghusband, E. (ed.), *Social Work and Social Values*, London: Allen and Unwin.

Horne, M. (1987), *Values in Social Work*, Aldershot: Wildwood House Ltd.

Horne, M. (1990), 'Is it social work?', in The Violence Against Children Study Group (eds.), *Taking Child Abuse Seriously*, London: Routledge.

Horne, M. (1995), 'Social Work and Time Travel: Language, Ethics and Individualism', in Glen, A. and Horne, M. (eds), *Commitment, Community and Social Work*, Ilkley: Bradford and Ilkley Community College.

Howe, D. (1979), 'Agency Function and Social Work Principles', *British Journal of Social Work*, 9 (1), pp. 29–47.

Howe, D. (1994), 'Modernity, Postmodernity and Social Work', *British Journal of Social Work*, 24 (5), pp. 513–32.

Howe, D. (1996), 'Surface and depth in social-work practice', in Parton, N. (ed.), *Social Theory, Social Change and Social Work*, London: Routledge.

Hugman, R. and Smith, D. (1995), *Ethical Issues in Social Work*, London: Routledge.

Husak, D. (1981), 'Paternalism and Autonomy', *Philosophy and Public Affairs*, 10, pp. 27–46.

Husband, C. (1995), 'The morally active practitioner and the ethics of anti-racist social work', in Hugman, R. and Smith, D. (eds) (1995), *Ethical Issues in Social Work*, London: Routledge.

Jamal, B. (1994), *Self Determination and Positive Freedom*, Norwich: UEA Social Work Monograph.

Jenkins, R. (1993), 'Incompetence and learning difficulties, anthropological perspectives', *Anthropology Today*, 9 (3), pp. 16–20.

Johnson, T.J. (1977), 'The Professions in the Class Structure', in Scase, R. (ed.), *Industrial Society, Class, Cleavage and Control*, London: Allen and Unwin.

Jones, H. (ed.) (1975), *Towards a New Social Work*, London: Routledge & Kegan Paul.

Jordan, B. (1984), 'The State isn't Abstract, it's a Social Worker Knocking on Someone's Door', *Social Work Today*, 3 September, pp. 10–14.

Jordan, B. (1990), *Social Work in an Unjust Society*, London: Harvester Wheatsheaf.

Jordan, B. (1991), 'Competencies and Values', *Social Work Education*, 10 (1), pp. 5–11.

Keith-Lucas, A. (1963), 'A Critique of the Principle of Client Self Determination', in McDermott, F.E. (ed.) (1975), *Self Determination in Social Work*, London: Routledge & Kegan Paul.

Lane, L.C. (1952), 'The Aggressive to Preventive Casework with Children's Problems', *Social Casework*, 33 (February).

Langan, M. and Lee, P. (eds) (1989), *Radical Social Work Today*, London: Unwin Hyman Ltd.

Levy, C.S. (1973), 'The Value Base of Social Work', *Journal of Education for Social Work*, 9, pp. 34–42.

Levy, C.S. (1976), *Social Work Ethics*, London: Human Science Press.

London Borough of Brent (1985), *A Child in Trust: Report of the panel of inquiry investigating the circumstances surrounding the death of Jasmine Beckford*, London Borough of Brent.

Lindley, R. (1984), 'Strategic Family Therapy and Respect for People', unpublished.

Lukes, S. (1973), *Individualism*, Oxford: Blackwell.

McDermott, F.E. (1975) (ed.), *Self Determination in Social Work*, London: Routledge & Kegan Paul.

McLeod, D. and Meyer, H.J. (1967), 'A Study of the Values of Social Workers', in Thomas, E.J. (ed.), *Behavioral Science for Social Workers*, New York: The Free Press.

Nokes, P. (1967), *The Professional Task in Welfare Practice*, London: Routledge & Kegan Paul.

Norman, A. (1980), *Rights and Risk – A Discussion Document on Civil Liberty in Old Age*, London: NCOP.

Oliver, M. (1990), *The Politics of Disablement*, Basingstoke: Macmillan.

Paton, H.J. (1948), *The Moral Law*, London: Hutchinson.

Parton, N. (1979), 'The natural history of child abuse: a study in social problem definition', *British Journal of Social Work*, 9 (4), pp. 431–51.

Parton, N. (1986), 'The Beckford Report: a critical appraisal', *British Journal of Social Work*, 16 (5), pp. 511–30.

Parton, N. (1994), '"Problematics of Government", (Post)modernity and Social Work', *British Journal of Social Work*, 24 (1), pp. 9–32.

Payne, M. (1985), 'The Code of Ethics, The Social Work Manager and the Organisation', in Watson, D. (ed.), *A Code of Ethics for Social Work, the 2nd Step*, London: Routledge & Kegan Paul.

Pearson, G. (1975a), *The Deviant Imagination*, London: Macmillan.

Pearson, G. (1975b), 'The Politics of Uncertainty: A Study in the Socialization of the Social Worker' in Jones, H. (ed.), *Towards a New Social Work*, London: Routledge & Kegan Paul.

Philp, M. (1979), 'Notes on the Form of Knowledge in Social Work', *Sociological Review*, 27, pp. 83–111.

Plant, R. (1970) *Social and Moral Theory in Casework*, London: Routledge & Kegan Paul.

Preston-Shoot, M. and Agass, D. (1990) *Making Sense of Social Work: Psychodynamics, Systems and Practice*, London: Macmillan.

Pritchard, C. and Taylor, R. (1978), *Social Work: Reform or Revolution?*, London: Routledge & Kegan Paul.

Pumphrey, M. (1959), *The Teaching of Values and Ethics in Social Work Education: A Project Report of the Curriculum Study*, Vol. XIII, US Council in Social Work Education.

Ragg, N. (1977), *People not Cases. A Philosophical Approach to Social Work*, London: Routledge & Kegan Paul.

Raynor, P. (1984), 'Evaluation with One Eye Closed: The Empiricist Agenda in Social Work Research', *British Journal of Social Work*, 14, pp. 1–10.

Reamer, F.G. (1982), *Ethical Dilemmas in Social Service*, New York: Columbia University Press.

Reamer, F.G. (1990), *Ethical Dilemmas in Social Service*, 2nd edn, New York: Columbia University Press.

Rogowski, S. (1991), 'Streetwise', *Social Work Today*, 27 June.

Ryan, J. and Thomas, F. (1980), *The Politics of Mental Handicap*, London: Penguin.

Scase, R. (ed.) (1977), *Industrial Society, Class, Cleavage and Control*, London: Allen and Unwin.

Secretary of State for Social Services (1988), *Report of the Inquiry into Child Abuse in Cleveland*, Cmnd 412, London: HMSO.

Seebohm Report, *Report of the Committee on Local Authority and Allied Social Services*, London: HMSO, 1968.

Simpkin, M. (1979), *Trapped Within Welfare*, London: Macmillan.

Smalley, R. (1967), *Theory for Social Work Practice*, New York: Columbia University Press.

Taylor, G. (1993), 'Challenges from the margins', in Clarke, J. (ed.) *A Crisis in care? Challenges to Social Work*, London: Sage Publications Ltd.

The Violence Against Children Study Group (1990), *Taking Child Abuse Seriously*, London: Routledge.

Thomas, E.J. (ed.) (1967), *Behavioural Science for Social Workers*, New York: The Free Press.

Timms, N. (1964), *Social Casework*, London: Routledge & Kegan Paul.

Timms, N. (1970), *Social Work: An Outline for Intending Students*, London: Routledge & Kegan Paul.

Timms, N. (ed.) (1980) *Social Welfare: Why and How*, London: Routledge & Kegan Paul.

Timms, N. (1983), *Social Work Values ... An Enquiry*, London: Routledge & Kegan Paul.

Timms, N. and Timms, R. (1977), *Perspectives in Social Work*, London: Routledge & Kegan Paul.

Timms, N. and Watson, D. (1978), *Philosophy in Social Work*, London: Routledge & Kegan Paul.

Titmuss, R.M. (1958), *Essays on the Welfare State*, London: Allen and Unwin.

Vigilante, J. (1974), 'Between Values and Science: Education for the Professional During a Moral Crisis or is Proof Truth?', *Journal of Education for Social Work*, 10, pp. 107–15.

Warham, J. (1977), *An Open Case: The Organisational Context of Social Work*, London: Routledge & Kegan Paul.

Warnock, M. (ed.) (1962), *Utilitarianism*, London: Collins.

Watson, D. (1980), *Caring for Strangers*, London: Routledge & Kegan Paul.

Watson, D. (ed.) (1985), *A Code of Ethics for Social Work, the 2nd Step*, London: Routledge & Kegan Paul.

Webb, S.A. and Mcbeath, G.B. (1989), 'A Political Critique of Kantian Ethics in Social Work', *British Journal of Social Work*, 19, pp. 491–506.

Whittington, K. (1975), 'Self-Determination Re-examined', in McDermott, F.E. (ed.), *Self Determination in Social Work*, London: Routledge & Kegan Paul.

Wilkes, R. (1981), *Social Work with Undervalued Groups*, London: Tavistock.

Williams, F. (1989), 'Mental handicap and oppression', in Brechin, A. and Swain, J. (eds), *Making Connections: reflecting on the lives and experiences of people with learning difficulties*, London: Hodder & Stoughton.

Winnicott, C. (1964), *Child Care and Social Work*, Welwyn: Codicote Press.

Younghusband, E. (ed.) (1967), *Social Work and Social Values*, London: Allen and Unwin.

Index